The
FINE Art
of
SMALL TALK

Advance Praise for *The Fine Art of Small Talk:*

In our business small talk is an essential leadership skill. Demonstrating conversational skills and techniques that build rapport and relationships in both social and business situations is a key to success.

Vice President, People Development
AMERUS Group

All the information she discussed can be used in personal life, as well as professional life.

Texas Dental Association

I realize from your material that "small talking" with people is a real and valid component of my job and of everyone's life. Small talk is a pleasure if you make it one, and trivial only if you think connecting with other human beings is trivial.

Dan Underwood
Vail Resort Ski Instructor

Your message is sure to not only be reflected in improved customer service — but also in people suddenly volunteering to go to the next corporate "mixer."

General Manager
Destination Services of Colorado, Inc.

I give my unqualified recommendation of this material to anyone in a group or practice seeking to gain useful and practical information in the art of communication.

S. Kent Lauson, DDS, MS
Aurora Orthodontics

The
Fine Art of
Small
Talk

Debra Fine

Published by Small Talk Publishers
Englewood, Colorado 80111

Publisher's Cataloging-in-Publication Data
Fine, Debra.
   The fine art of small talk / Debra Fine. —1st Ed. —Englewood, CO : Small Talk Publishers, 2002.

        p.   ;   cm.
   ISBN 0-9711322-0-8

   1. Conversation. 2. Oral communication. I. Title.

BJ2121. F56   2002   2002101183
177.2   —dc21   CIP

www.DebraFine.com
Printed in the United States of America

06 05 04 03   • 5

Foreword

W hen I first got into the business of helping people cultivate conversation skills, I ran into a lot of skepticism. Invariably, executives would scoff at the idea as a housewife's trivial initiative to overcome boredom. Then I would get clandestine calls for assistance from folks with prestigious titles. People would construct elaborate covert operations to seek advice without actually asking for it. Turns out that people were embarrassed about it. I can appreciate that. In a previous life as a nerdy engineer, I was burdened by poor social skills and embarrassed by my own conversational ineptitude. Before I gave myself a remedial education in the Fine Art of SmallTalk, I had been a poor communicator and a timid person for as long as I could recall.

As a girl I had been overweight, a reticent kid who sat invisible in the back of the class, often excluded because of my size. One of my most vivid memories of childhood is that of a birthday party for my third-grade classmate, Rita. Every girl in my class was invited except for one other very overweight girl and me. That experience was so hurtful that I withdrew into a world of books. I had no idea how to make a friend or have a friend. Consequently, I never learned how to talk to my peers.

Naturally, when I got older, I selected a career without a high demand for conversation. I became an engineer — a perfect choice, since engineering tends to be highly technical and requires little chatting. I routinely made technical presentations or answered complex engineering questions without any trouble. All that was required was competence in my field. However, when I was sent to conferences or industry meetings, I was expected to mingle with colleagues. Network. Meet clients. I was filled with panic. I only knew one way to start a conversation. Without fail, I would ask every person I met, "What do you do?" After we exchanged career notes, the conversation invariably sputtered to an agonizing halt. I didn't know how to keep it going. I skipped every social function I could. The ones I couldn't, I'd arrive late, leave early and, in between, pray that some other person with better skills and a kind heart would rescue me by initiating a conversation.

I struggled with the art of conversation throughout my tenure as an engineer. Then I took a break from my career to have my two children. In that interlude, I decided that I was weary of being overweight and self-conscious. I lost 65 pounds. My self-image improved. I wanted to have friends and to have fun. To do so, I knew that I would have to acquire better social skills. I took note of others who were successful at cultivating friendships and mingling in a crowd. I watched their techniques and began timidly to try to imitate them.

My motivation went into overdrive after my husband and I divorced. I realized that I'd have to start socializing if I wanted to meet anyone. Here I was approaching 40 years of age, having been out of my field for a number of years and needing to meet people. It was a daunting prospect, to say the least. But I realized that acquiring conversation skills wasn't rocket science. I convinced myself it couldn't be that tough or I wouldn't see so many people doing it so well. I made it my goal to figure out how to keep a conversation going for longer than five minutes.

One of my first experiments with small talk was a life-changing success. I went to happy hour at a local nightspot with a girlfriend. A man across the room began making eye contact with me. All night we kept exchanging glances, never speaking. My girlfriend prodded me, "Debra," she said, "just go over there and say something to him."

I replied, "Oh, I don't know. I don't have anything to say. Besides, if he wanted to meet me, he'd have come over by now."

But my girlfriend would not relent. She was so adamant that her challenge finally inspired me to go over and say something to him. As I walked across the room, my heart pounded so loudly, I could hardly hear myself say hello to the man I now know as Rex. He pulled out a chair and said he was delighted to meet me. From that inauspicious beginning we began to date each other. A friendship developed, and I learned a lot about Rex. The most important thing I came to learn, though, was why Rex hadn't approached me first at the happy hour. I was certain that his reluctance was an unspoken commentary on some fault of mine. It had to be that I was too tall, that I still weighed too much, or that I just wasn't his type. I could not have been more wrong. It wasn't about me at all. It was about him. He was too shy to approach me.

I couldn't believe it. It really turned my thinking around. For the first time, I understood that there were lots of talented, educated, wonderful people in the world who are incredibly shy. I realized that if my girlfriend hadn't insisted, and if I hadn't found my courage, I never would have met a man who became an integral part of my life. No, I didn't marry him, but he did become one of my closest friends.

That experience made me a convert to small talk. I finally

understood how great a tool it is for building rapport with people. I devoted myself to learning about it, practicing it and helping others become good at it. I started my business, The Fine Art of SmallTalk, and have been small talking my way around the country ever since. I have met countless fascinating people and made many friends. My life is now richly populated with diverse individuals who bring added meaning and depth to each of my days.

My goal in writing this book is to offer what I've learned so that you can reap the rewards that come from having a repertoire of conversation skills. The techniques, tips, and skills in this book are for everyone — not just nerds. I know salespeople who are wonderful at making formal presentations but who enter a networking event in a cold sweat. I've met teachers who can chat with students and colleagues but have no idea what to say to parents at school functions. Harried, yet happy, stay-at-home moms are a bundle of entertainment at a play group but walk away from a Junior League meeting or church event feeling isolated and disconnected. I know one physician who closed his practice and joined an HMO because, despite his expertise as a healer, he lacked the conversation skills and confidence to garner new referrals. The list goes on. Competent people from all walks of life need assistance to develop conversation skills.

This book will provide you those small-talk skills. There is no doubt that enhancing your conversational skills will improve your quality of life. I think you'll be surprised at the potency of small talk. It has an amazing ripple effect. Becoming a good conversationalist will bring new people into your network of friends and colleagues. You will find joy in the social events you used to dread, and you will create pathways and channels for new opportunities to present themselves.

Take a moment. Spend some time filling out the following **"Winning at SmallTalk"** worksheet. If you answer yes to most, you are certainly on the right track. If you find yourself responding no to more than a few, it's time to get to work.

Winning at Small Talk

Please answer Yes or No to the following questions:

1. I have joined or participated in at least one club or group activity to develop new business, personal, or romantic friendships this year. ☐ Yes ☐ No

2. I'm conscious of "taking turns" in most conversations so that I can learn more about others and help them get to know me. ☐ Yes ☐ No

3. In the past year, I have used my contacts to help at least two people find a new job, get a date, hook up with potential customers and clients, or I have provided information for other networking purposes. ☐ Yes ☐ No

4. I go to at least two functions a month where I can meet people in my profession/industry or who are potential decision-makers. ☐ Yes ☐ No

5. If someone is friendly toward
   me it is easy to be friendly back.
   However, I don't wait to make
   sure someone is friendly before
   I am friendly toward him or her.   ☐ Yes ☐ No

6. When someone asks me,
   "What's new?" instead of saying,
   "Not much," I often talk about
   something exciting in my life.   ☐ Yes ☐ No

7. At meetings, parties, etc., I
   introduce myself to people I don't
   know and come away knowing
   the names of at least three
   new people.   ☐ Yes ☐ No

Well, how did you do? All right — that's enough small talking — let's get down to business!

Dedicated with love
to the wind beneath my wings,
Steve Tilliss,

and my two magnificent
sources of inspiration,
Jared Holst and Sarah Holst.

Table of Contents

What's the Big Deal About Small Talk?

You pull into the parking lot, turn off the engine, and sit for a minute dreading the next two hours. An important client has invited you to an open house in celebration of their new downtown office. You hate these things: You don't know what to say, you don't know anyone except the client, and you always feel like you're trying not to look lost, so you eat and drink more than you should, just to stay occupied. You must attend — that's a given — but you sink deeper into the front seat and agonize over how long you should stay. Does dropping by for 30 minutes do the trick, or will you insult one of your best clients if you don't stay for the whole event? You search for excuses to get yourself out of there early. You could have someone page you at a specified time with a supposed emergency; perhaps one of the kids has a big game; or maybe you'll just allow your anxiety to carry you right into an illness.

Casual conversation happens at least a dozen times a day — on the way into the office, picking up your daughter from soccer practice, riding the elevator with a colleague, fielding a phone call from your mother-in-law, attending an industry meeting, taking a client to lunch, going to a job interview – the list is endless! Yet for some of us, these demands for small talk don't ever make small talk any easier. If anything, such encounters increase anxiety and cause some people to dread social events, business lunches, and chance encounters with neighbors.

If your conversations evaporate almost as soon as they've begun, or if you're a reluctant participant at social and business get-togethers, you've come to the right place. This book will help you attain the conversation skills you need to feel confident and poised in any situation. If you practice the simple techniques revealed in the book, you'll put your conversational demons behind you. You will learn how to:

- **Engage any individual in a meaningful dialogue**

- **Rejuvenate a dying conversation**

- **Transition into new topics**

- **Feel more at ease at networking events, parties, and receptions**

- **Develop business friendships**

- **Step out of a conversation with grace**

Getting to the big stuff

Small talk has a bad rap as the lowly stepchild of *real conversation*, yet it serves an extremely important function. Without it, you rarely get to the *real conversation*. Small talk is the icebreaker that clears the way for more intimate conversation, laying the foundation for a stronger relationship. People who excel at small talk are experts at making others feel included, valued, and comfortable. And that goes a long way toward furthering a business relationship, closing a deal, opening the door for romance, or making a friend.

The good news about conversation skills is that anyone can learn them. Don't be fooled into thinking that all those other people you see who are smiling and happily mingling come by it naturally. Sure, some are natural-born talkers, but most have had to work at it. They've practiced, attended seminars, hired personal coaches, and read books. You don't think so? Trust me, I know. I used to be a geeky, introverted engineer — no one has worse skills than I once did. I became a pro by learning the skills and then practicing them. It's that simple.

The first step is to let go of the idea that we are all somehow supposed to know how to converse with strangers and acquaintances. It's simply not true. We are not taught how to do it, nor is there some biological mechanism that instinctively takes over when we find ourselves in a conversational quandary.

Mark McCormack, an attorney from Cleveland who founded one of the first sports management firms in the United States, once said, "All things being equal, people will buy from a friend. All things being not quite so equal, people will still buy from a friend." The bottom line: It's to your benefit to cultivate friendships, not collect business cards.

In his book *Megatrends*, John Naisbitt talks about our high-tech/high-touch world: "The more technology around us, the more need for human touch." People are compensating for living in the high-tech world of computers, e-mail, and entrepreneurial work settings by reaching out to other people. Witness the fact that shopping malls are the third most frequented places in America! People need to gather, to connect. If you make the extra effort to connect with people, you are extending a hand that is usually received very warmly.

Talk is cheap...but very valuable

Small talk is essential to creating and enriching business relationships. Always begin and end your business conversation with small talk to humanize the relationship. Investors choose financial planners as much for their ability to make them feel secure and comfortable as they do for their financial savvy. How important is your physician's bedside manner to you? Hairstylists are the consummate conversationalists. They understand that no woman will spend the better part of an hour or more sitting in a chair at the mercy of someone with a sharp instrument unless she feels comfortable!

In an indirect but very important way, small talk relates to how businesses and individuals spend money. In general, people and organizations spend money for two reasons:

1. **To solve a problem or fill a need.**

   Think about it. You dash into a fast-food restaurant for lunch so you can spare yourself from packing leftovers. You hire a babysitter so you can escape for an evening out. You pay a lawn care company to cut your grass so that you can enjoy more free time and fewer allergy symptoms.

2. **To gain good, positive feelings.**

   My neighbor Susan continues banking with the same institution even though another bank in her neighborhood offers a better free-checking deal — because she likes the people. My friend Vince moved to the opposite side of town and still drives back to the old neighborhood to take his dog to the vet. Although he and the vet do not socialize together, he can't imagine going anywhere else. He likes that particular vet.

A good conversationalist frequently evokes the positive feelings that people long to have; and the reality is that buyers' choices about where to spend their money are influenced by the presence or absence of rapport. Small talk is a big deal because it is integral to establishing rapport. Parents and teachers visit before a conference to create a bond. Mortgage brokers chat with referral sources like title companies and realtors to strengthen the relationship and garner business.

It's a tough and fast world. The news media provides more bad news than good. People appreciate a conversation in which they feel acknowledged, heard, and significant. While it's understood that people seek these benefits in conversations with friends, it's also true that people choose to buy goods and services from individuals perceived as warm, friendly, and caring. From the senior executive of a large corporation selecting a supplier, to a parent picking up a few groceries, to the account executive calling a courier — buying decisions are all influenced by the rapport they've established with the other party.

Garner big gains with a little talking

Effective managers use small talk at the front end of a meeting to set the tone for discussion and to create a bridge to more meaningful, and perhaps difficult, dialogue. Casual conversation and informal icebreakers offer opportunities to build rapport, create a cohesive team and increase the chances of success.

By developing your conversation skills, you can even improve communication with your children. You'll recognize the most repeated question in parenting — *"How was school?"* — as a conversation killer. You can avoid the usual one-word response — *"Fine"* — and instead create a dialogue. Imagine: You may actually gain insight into what they're learning and who their friends are!

Small talk is no small thing. It's a valuable personal and professional thread that connects people. Appreciating the power of small talk is the first step. By recognizing its value, you'll be more inclined to acquire the skills. If you thought small talk was all about becoming a smooth-talking used-car salesperson, you were mistaken. Small talk is the verbal equivalent of that first domino: It starts a chain reaction with all kinds of implications for your life.

This book is filled with techniques and hints to give you the skills to enjoy the perks of quality conversation. You won't necessarily decide that you love networking events or cocktail parties, but you will have the skills to be successful at them. Like me, you may still prefer to stay at home with a good book rather than attend an event where you don't know anyone. There's no denying that it takes effort to mingle at an open house when the room is full of strangers. However, there's also no denying that there are plenty of events we're expected to attend. So it makes sense to maximize your opportunities, and improved conversation skills will do just that. By the time you finish this book, you'll have the information and resources at your disposal to make you a successful conversationalist at any function. Improving your conversation skills can enhance your leadership abilities, reduce your anxiety in social situations, boost your confidence, lead you to new friendships and more. Before you know it, you might actually enjoy talking!

Get Over Your Mom's Good Intentions

It's no wonder so many of us lack adequate conversation skills. Some of our oldest memories still haunt and influence us as adults. Because of our earliest training, we are predisposed to refrain from initiating a conversation. When we were impressionable toddlers, our parents taught us:

- Good things come to those who wait

- Silence is golden

- Wait to be properly introduced

- Don't talk to strangers

Those messages served us well as kids; the advice helped ensure our safety and taught us manners. But now, as adults, our safety isn't at stake with every new person we meet! And by now our manners are well established. The time has come to replace those old messages with more relevant advice. Here it is.

In safe situations, make it a point to talk to strangers

To expand your circle of friends and colleagues, you must start engaging strangers and acquaintances in conversation. There is no other way. Strangers have the potential to become good friends, long-term clients, valued associates, and bridges to new experiences and other people. Start thinking of strangers as people who can bring new dimensions to your life, not as persons to be feared.

Introduce yourself

When was the last time someone properly introduced you to another person? The truth is that the host of a gathering rarely takes the time to do so in a meaningful way. You've been to this kind of event. You go to a holiday open house hosted by an important client. The client greets you, takes your coat, visits for a minute, and shows you to the food. Your client departs to greet another guest, and you are left standing next to the shrimp cocktail, not knowing a single person in the room. If you wait for the host to come back and properly introduce you to some of the other guests, chances are your only new encounter will be with the shrimp. Times have changed: People expect you to mingle on your own, introduce yourself, and take the initiative to get acquainted. As Babe Ruth said, "Don't let the fear of striking out get in your way." Remember, even your closest confidante was once a stranger. Take the risk. Walk up to someone and introduce yourself. Extend your hand, make eye contact, and smile saying, "Hello. My name is Deb Fine. It's nice to meet you." If you are a member of an association, chamber of commerce, fraternity or sorority, church or synagogue, you are probably aware of these organizations' constant challenge of retaining membership. We join such organizations seeking out fellowship; we often leave or quit because we don't find it. Instead, we perceive others as groups or cliques that won't let us join. I think most of us can relate to the following poem, author unknown:

Thoughts from a New Member

I see you at the meetings,
but you never say hello.

You're busy all the time you're there
with those you really know.

I sit among the members,
yet I'm a lonely gal.

The new ones feel as strange as I;
the old ones pass us by.

Darn it, you folks urged us to join
and talked of fellowship,

You could just cross the room, you know,
but you never make the trip.

Can't you just nod your head and smile
or stop and shake a hand,

Then go sit among your friends?
Now that I'd understand.

I'll be at your next meeting,
and hope that you will spend

The time to introduce yourself,
I joined to be your friend.

At your next opportunity to spend time at a reception, coffee break, hospitality room, or wedding, look around the room. Find that approachable person and include them in conversation.

Silence is impolite

Spare yourself some pain and forget the adage that silence is golden. I first recognized the downside of silence while I was working as an engineer, side by side with a peer who had the same academic credentials, tenure, and work quality. We were considered equals in every sense of the word. However, my colleague was outgoing and conversational. Staff members in marketing, human resources, and quality knew her name, as did executives at corporate headquarters. Our immediate supervisor noticed her and commented frequently on her work. When the time came for a promotion, she got it and I didn't. I simply wasn't as visible because I was so silent.

I later learned another costly lesson about silence. My friend, Johnnie, a regional director with a Fortune 100 company, dragged me to all her company functions. Her boss, Bob, a senior vice president, attended these functions, too. I admired his poise and grace as he easily conversed with everyone. Bob's self-confidence intimidated me so much that I rarely talked with him, despite my respect for him. Even when he approached me, I was too nervous to say much.

When I moved into engineering sales, I called on Bob to reintroduce myself and promote my employer's services. Before I could even finish introducing myself, Bob blasted me, saying, "I can't believe that you're calling me. We've been at the same parties a dozen times, and you've ignored me at every one. You're the biggest snob I know. I have no interest in buying anything from you." Needless to say, I was stunned and horrified by his reaction. It had never occurred to me that shyness could be mistaken for arrogance. While shyness and arrogance are worlds apart, the visible manifestation of each can appear the same. People generally do not give others the benefit of the doubt in this regard. Don't be mistaken as haughty or pretentious by keeping silent; it can cost you dearly. Start small talking and let others see your personality. You know how much you appreciate the efforts others put forth in conversation. Make the same effort. Contrary to what your elders taught you, silence is not golden.

Good things come to those who go get them!

Waiting will net you a bunch of lost time. You have to take the initiative. Don't spend another minute thinking that if you just keep waiting, interesting people will introduce themselves. It's not going to happen. Out of habit, and to make things easy on ourselves, we seek out someone we know — a colleague, a client, even a competitor. We are comfortable with these people because they attend the same functions, know the same jargon, and are trying to reach the same decision-makers. We end up paying $40 to attend an event and then seek out people we already know because it's less threatening. Yet the purpose of the event was to make new contacts.

If ever there was a place you'd expect people to mingle, it's a singles event. Yet they are notorious for attracting more wallflowers than a convention of periodontists! (I can say this because my husband is a periodontist.) Most people at singles events — including myself in a former life — spend most of their time uncomfortably waiting around and scanning the crowd for a friend. When a friend appears, they immediately spend the evening hanging out together. If they wanted to be with one another, why didn't they just go out on a date? If they don't want to date each other, what are they doing spending the evening together? They're talking! Yes, talking — it's easy, comfortable, and safe. It is, however, no way to meet a new person and spark a romance!

Good things come to those who take action and start creating good things. American movie star, commentator, and folk legend Will Rogers nailed it when he said, "Go out on a limb. That's where all the fruit is." Although it might be scary to climb out from the safety of the trunk, you'll rarely pluck sweet fruit waiting there.

It's up to you to start a conversation

Do you know the biggest social fear in America? It's public speaking. And do you know the second? It's fear of starting a conversation with a stranger. So remember when you walk into a luncheon or a cocktail party, most people there are scared to death to talk to you. Fear of rejection keeps many of us from risking conversation, but the probability of rejection is actually quite small. In the unlikely event that your efforts are unappreciated, remember that it's doubtful you'll ever see that person again. You will be the hero if you start the conversation. You will gain stature, respect, and rapport if you can get the conversation going. Almost always, people will embrace your efforts and appreciate your leadership.

It's up to you to assume the burden of conversation

If you generally wait for someone else to take the initiative in a conversation, you have been self-centered. It's true! You have allowed your own comfort to take precedence over every other person's. You haven't been doing your fair share of the work. If you've largely ignored your conversational responsibilities, it's time to take ownership. You cannot rely on the other person to carry the conversation for you — a monologue is a chore and seldom very interesting. Furthermore, one-word answers to questions do not count as shouldering your share of the burden.

The first step in becoming a great conversationalist is becoming invested in the conversation and actively working to help the other person feel comfortable. Take a look at the list of icebreaker questions that follow and make a commitment to use at least four of them in your next conversation. If you're afraid you won't remember them, write them down, put them in your pocket, and refer to them before you to go into the event. If you go blank while you're there, excuse yourself for a moment and walk into the restroom to take a peek at your list. The most famous and worn-out icebreaker is that age-old question, "What do you do for a living?" It's so standard that it didn't make the icebreaker list. Here are some other ways to begin a conversation that will provide a refreshing diversion from shoptalk. Be prepared to reciprocate, since your conversation partner is likely to return whatever questions you pose.

Icebreakers

1. What is a typical day like for you?

2. If you could move anywhere in the world tomorrow, where would you move? Why?

3. What was the best job you ever had? What was the worst?

4. Tell me about the best vacation you've ever taken.

5. What's your favorite thing to do on a rainy day?

6. If you could replay any moment in your life, what would it be?

7. What one thing would you really like to own? Why?

8. If you learned that you were gong to die tomorrow, what would be the one thing you'd most regret not doing?

9. What was it like in the town where you grew up?

10. What would you like to come back as in your next life?

11. What do you think is the perfect age? Why?

12. Of all the places that you've lived, tell me about the one you like the best.

Icebreakers

13. What's your favorite holiday? What do you enjoy about it?

14. What are some of your family traditions that you particularly enjoy?

15. Tell me about the first car you ever bought.

16. Who were your idols as kid? Have they changed?

17. Describe a memorable teacher you had.

18. Tell me about a movie/book that you've seen or read more than once.

19. What's your favorite restaurant? Why?

20. Tell me why you were named _____. What is the origin of your last name?

21. Tell me about a place that you've visited that you hope never to return to.

22. What's the best surprise you've ever received?

23. What's the neatest surprise you've ever planned and pulled off for someone else?

24. Skiing here is always challenging. What are some of your favorite places to ski?

Icebreakers

25. Who would star as you in a movie about your life? Why that person?

26. Who is the most famous person you've met?

27. What's the most anti-establishment thing you ever did?

28. Describe a costume that you wore to a party.

29. Are you alone by choice or by chance?

30. Tell me about a political position you'd like to hold.

31. What song reminds you of an incident in your life?

32. What's the most memorable meal you've eaten?

33. What's the most memorable coincidence you've experienced or heard about?

34. How are you able to tell if that melon is ripe?

35. What motion picture star would you like to interview? Why?

36. Tell me about your family.

37. What aroma brings forth a special memory?

Icebreakers

38. Describe the scariest person you ever met.

39. What's your favorite thing to do alone?

40. Tell about a childhood friend who used to get you in trouble.

41. Tell about a time that you had too much to eat or drink.

42. Describe your first away-from-home living quarters or experience.

43. What's your fantasy of a romantic evening?

44. Tell me about a time that you lost a job.

45. Share a memory of one of your grandparents.

46. Describe an embarrassing moment you've had.

47. Tell me something most would never guess about you.

48. What would you do if you won a million dollars?

49. What's the most difficult part of your job?

50. How has the Internet affected your life?

Take the Plunge: Start a Conversation!

You are armed with a pocketful of icebreakers. You know that if someone else greets you, you've got some great material for a conversation. Just having topics in mind to talk about goes a long way toward improving your skills. However, there are still a few gaps that can give you needless heart palpitations. Right now you only feel prepared to respond when someone else engages you in conversation. So you walk into your son's school and wait for another parent to say hello. You go to an industry dinner and try to act busy while you hope for a colleague to come along and talk. No. No. No. It does not need to be so stressful.

You can start the conversation — yes, *you!* It's not nearly as hard as you think. And the best part is that it puts you in charge of your own destiny. Instead of waiting for someone — anyone — to talk to you, you choose your conversation partner. What a concept: You get to select someone. You might even enjoy it!

The rules are simple. When someone gives you a smile, you are naturally inclined to smile back. Be the first to smile and greet another person. That's pretty easy. Just a smile and a few words, and it's done. Be sure that you make eye contact. That simple act is the beginning of establishing rapport. In those few seconds you have shown an interest in the other person. However, if the thought of this makes you want to jump into bed and pull the covers over your head, practice flashing your pearly whites in a setting that requires nothing further. Walk through the mall and just say hello to ten people as you pass them. As you cut through the parking lot into the grocery store, greet three other shoppers. Keep practicing until it feels natural.

What's in a name?

Okay, now you actually do have to stay and talk, not just offer a passing hello. Make it a point to remember the other person's name; learning and using names is probably the single most important rule of good conversation, so stay focused during the introduction. Repeat the name back in your greeting, "Nice to meet you, Debra." To help yourself commit the name to memory, immediately use the person's name in the conversation. Refrain from thinking about your reply and concentrate on the other person's name. Focus on the name, repeat it, and then formulate your answer.

If you do get distracted during the introduction and miss the name, confess! Don't go through the whole conversation pretending that you know the person's name. It's better to say something like, "Excuse me, I'm not sure I got your name." It is always preferable to have the other party repeat it than to fake it. Never, ever fake it! This is especially true if, for example, you run into someone you've met previously whose name you cannot recall as you are standing in line at the movie theater. Don't wait for divine inspiration. Say, "I'm so sorry. I've forgotten your name. Please remind me."

You no longer have to worry about avoiding people because you've forgotten their names. Assume the burden, tell the truth, and chances are you'll go on to have a very pleasant conversation. Even if you're on the other side of a crowded room or passing in the grocery store, go over and greet the person. If you avoid someone because you are embarrassed over having forgotten her name, you've just compounded the error with rudeness.

Individuals with foreign or unusual names get slighted more than the rest of us. Make it a point to learn the proper pronunciation, even if it means that the other person repeats it a few times. When you take the time to learn another person's name, you are expressing a sincere interest in that individual that will be warmly received. Conversely, if you get lazy because a person has a difficult name, you are sending a message that it's not worth your trouble to learn his name.

Remembering names is well worth the effort. In fact, learning names is part of hosting the conversation. A host is always expected to know and use every person's name, since the host is responsible for making introductions as new individuals enter the conversation. I was seated at a table for eight and met three people who had arrived at the table before I did. As others arrived, I extended my hand, introduced myself and made the introductions to the other three. I said, "This is Linda with Sun Microsystems, and Jon with Lucent Technologies, and Sam from the Association of Safety Engineers." Acting as the host puts everyone at ease and creates an atmosphere of warmth and appreciation that naturally encourages conversation. It also positions you as a leader in the group.

Nix the nicknames

If a colleague introduces himself as "Michael," don't call him "Mike." If he wanted you to call him "Mike," he would have introduced himself that way. If someone has a difficult name, make the effort to learn it — do not shorten it to a nickname without permission! When someone shortens my name to "Debbie," it makes me crazy.

I know I'm not alone in this. After a meeting, a woman named Julia walked up to me and said, "Debra, I've always wanted to tell you something. My name used to be Debra, also. I used to give presentations for the government. Invariably, someone would call me Debbie while asking a question. I hate the name Debbie. Finally, I just couldn't stand it anymore. I changed my name to Julia!"

Make sure you use people's names and get them right! For instance, I call a client whose secretary answers, "Katherine Winter's office, this is Susan." I respond by saying, "Hi Susan. This is Debra Fine. May I speak with Katherine?" Notice that I used each person's name, and I did not take liberties with any of them. Susan is very important because she represents the gateway to my client. It would not serve me to annoy her by slashing her name to "Sue," nor would it be helpful to avoid using her name altogether. Using people's names shows that you are interested in them and makes them feel special.

Another example: I was at the video store returning a couple of overdue movies. I started talking to the clerk while we were waiting for the computer. In the course of our brief conversation I used his name and asked if had seen every movie in the store. By the time my late fees showed up on-screen, he cancelled them and told me to have a nice day! When you use another person's name sincerely in a conversation, it makes that person feel special.

It's better to give than to receive

It's just as important to give your name when you meet someone — even if you've met him or her previously and think they should remember your name. Consider it a random act of kindness. Extend your hand: "Hi, Patrick, Debra Fine. How are you?" By stating my name, I let Patrick off the hook. If he had forgotten my name, it didn't show, and he didn't have to waste conversation time being distracted trying to recall my name.

My husband is a periodontist. As a group, periodontists are not known for their charm or gregarious personalities. Frequently, when we go out, his patients recognize him and start a conversation without reintroducing themselves. My husband doesn't have a clue who they are and feels awkward. He can't include me in the conversation easily because he can't get through the introductions. Don't ever assume that someone who sees you infrequently will remember your name — especially when they see you out of context. You will remember the realtor who spent a Sunday driving you around looking at houses easier than she will — especially if you are in sweats at the gas station. Cut her some slack; offer your name when you say hello.

Keep the Conversation Going!

Remember: Instead of sitting back and waiting for another kind soul to start a conversation, take the lead. Think of it as if you invited that person to your home for dinner. As host, it's your job to see that your guest is comfortable. The same is true in conversation — try to make your guest as comfortable as possible. When you walk into a party or a gathering, find a person to meet. It's much easier to engage one person rather than enter a group conversation, so begin by looking for the "approachable person."

The approachable person is one who makes eye contact with you or who is not actively engaged in a conversation. It's the person getting a bite to eat, someone sitting alone at a table, or the one crossing the room unescorted. More often than not, these people are relieved to have someone else initiates the conversation. Believe me, I've been around plenty of these folks — they are intelligent, interesting, welcoming…and shy. They are in the same spot you were before you decided to improve your skills. If you take the conversational plunge, they will herald you as a savior.

Make it a point to look around a room when you first enter it. It doesn't matter what the event is — a meeting, a reception, a baby shower, a party — even a family reunion — there are people standing alone or sitting at an empty table. Don't wait; make eye contact and be the first to smile. You'll net a smile back, and you'll put the other person at ease, they way any fine host would! People will reward you by being attentive listeners and giving you a chance to practice your icebreakers.

Not only are icebreakers a good way to start a conversation, but some of the statements are accompanied by questions you can ask to keep the ball rolling. Don't use a statement alone. Using a statement by itself is like lobbing the conversational ball blindfolded, not knowing where it will land or whether it will get tossed back. For example, enthusiastic exclamations like, *What a beautiful day*, or *That was a great* _____, are indirect invitations to chat. Better to be direct, so there is no doubt you are starting a dialogue. Try these:

Starting with Statements

- What a beautiful day. What is your favorite thing about spring?

- I was truly touched by that movie. How did you like it? Why?

- This is a wonderful restaurant. What is your favorite restaurant? Why?

- What a great conference! Tell me about the sessions you attended.

- I was absent last week. Describe what went on...

Starting with Statements

- That was an interesting program after lunch. What did you think?

- Presidential campaigns seem to start immediately after the inauguration. What do you think of the campaign process?

- I am so frustrated with getting this business off the ground. Do you have any ideas?

- I am excited about our new mayor. How do you think her administration will be different from her predecessor's?

- Your lawn always looks so green. What is your secret?

- We've been working together for months now. I'd like to get to know you better. Tell me about some of your outside interests.

- You worked pretty hard on that stair stepper. What other equipment do you use?

- You always wear such attractive clothes. Do you have some favorite places to shop?

- How do you manage to run a house with four children?

- I read in the newspaper that our governor has taken another trip overseas. What do you think of all his travel?

Party of five

It's tough for a conversational novice to break into a group of five or more. A group this size is usually well entrenched, and it requires covert operations to infiltrate the group. Use these tactics when you find it necessary or desirable to get engaged with these folks:

- **Show interest in the speaker, but stand slightly away from the group.** A group this size is slow to warm so first let them become accustomed to seeing you. Slowly, they will shift to bring you into the circle.

- **Ease into the group by demonstrating that you've been listening.** Look for welcoming signs such as them asking your opinion or physically shifting positions to better include you.

- **Initially, it is best to find a point of agreement; barring that, just acknowledge the speaker.** Wait before rocking the boat with a big wave of radical opinions. Before offering your views, let the group warm to you. If you come on too strong too fast, the group will resent your intrusion and disband. Then you have to start all over again, looking to chat with someone you haven't just offended!

Like most things that are unfamiliar, starting a conversation appears harder than it actually is. If you still feel uncertain, listen to this true story. A national news show put a hidden microphone on a gentleman and set him loose at a party. His mission was to start as many conversations with women as possible using the ridiculous icebreaker, "Hi. What's your sign?" Here we are in a new millennium, and he was using that infamous 1970's line! And it worked! He walked up to a woman, smiled and spoke his line. She responded by saying, "Taurus. What's yours?"

He answered with, "Libra. Do you know much about astrology?" They went on to have a very interesting conversation. The moral of the story is that it's the effort that counts. What matters is taking the plunge and starting the conversation. This gentleman was successful because he showed an interest in what the other person had to say, and she was open to it. Showing genuine interest is flattering and essential to conversing. If you are interested in how I lost 65 pounds or how I started my business or anything else about me, I feel special. I also think positively about you and want to continue talking with you. The more interest you show in me, the more interesting you become to me. The simple act of truly being interested in the other person has an amazing effect on the conversation — it just snowballs!

You will be successful if you just take the initiative and give it a try. You'll be surprised by how easy it is and at the positive reinforcement you get from people when you start a conversation. Remember the following four steps and you are well on your way to an excellent chat:

1. Smile.

2. Make eye contact.

3. Find that approachable person!

4. Offer your name and use theirs.

Give it a try. You'll discover that it's really worthwhile. The true effort is taking the risk to be the first to say hello. There is no perfect icebreaker. "What's your sign?" is a huge risk as an icebreaker. As silly as it was, it worked because the woman decided she would allow the man to engage her in conversation. Think about it. We all do that. We size someone up, determine if we are in the mood to chat, and gauge whether it is worth the investment of time to chat with the approaching person. The person being approached has already decided on their willingness to respond — regardless of the words said.

Often, people make the huge mistake of assuming they will have nothing in common with another person. We easily allow differences of all kinds to bias us against engaging in conversation. We allow gender, ethnicity, social status, generation, occupation, lifestyle, and a host of other differences to create artificial barriers to success. In the course of touring the country and talking to thousands of people in every geographic region, from all walks of life, I have affirmed that we are all more alike than we are different. It's simply a matter of talking, showing an interest, and listening. When I approach a conversation I'm slowly peeling an onion: Just one layer at a time. I am always amazed and gratified by how interesting and worthwhile it is to take the time to talk with a stranger.

At one of the first programs I presented, I asked everyone to introduce himself or herself and tell why they came to a session on small talk. The first person to introduce himself was a gentleman named Bob. He said he was attending because he was a Motorola customer-service engineer, and his boss wanted him to improve his conversational skills with customers. He added that, although his boss sent him to the session, he was glad because he'd just moved to the very small town of Elizabeth, Colorado. As a single man alone, he felt isolated and wanted to meet people. Here's what followed:

Elizabeth, Colorado, Bob. I used to live in Elizabeth. I lived next to the Douglas County line near the town of Parker. Are you there or closer to the town of Elizabeth itself?

No, I live near Parker, as well, in a development called Ponderosa Park Estates.

Ponderosa Park Estates? Wow. Bob, I used to live there, too! I lived right near Ponderosa Lane and Overlook Road.

Well, Debra, I live on Overlook Road.

That is amazing, Bob. I lived in the log house at 120 Overlook Road.

Well, Debra, this is truly amazing because I live in the log house at 120 Overlook Road!

It turns out that the family to whom my ex-husband and I sold the home in 1985 moved, and they sold it to Bob in 1991. Because of this chance encounter, and because I took an interest in the fact that Bob was from Elizabeth, Bob invited me to bring my family to see the house again. I was delighted. We visited Bob at his house, and my kids got the chance to experience a part of their own history that would otherwise have been lost to them since they were too young to remember having lived there.

Make the effort, and you'll be richly rewarded. You have a jumbo-sized list of icebreakers to get you started, and "What's your sign?" isn't even on the list!

Let's Give 'Em Something to Talk About

Y ou've smiled, made eye contact, found the approachable person, offered your name and used theirs.
What's left, you ask? Plenty! Have no fear — this is
where it really gets fun. If you are introverted, you will love
this part because you stay on the quiet side. Your mission is
to get your conversation partners talking about themselves.
Most people enjoy the opportunity to share their stories,
and if you give them the chance, they'll start talking. This is
a no-brainer route to small-talking success.

It's all in the asking

By asking open-ended questions, you offer your conversation partner the opportunity to disclose as much or as little
as she wants. These questions demand more than a simple
yes or no answer, yet they make no stressful demands. Your
partner will decide how much she feels comfortable saying.
Such questions are effective with co-workers, kids, neighbors, in-laws, industry colleagues, friends, and when first
making the acquaintance of a stranger. The key to success-

fully using open-ended questions is choosing the right question and then following up with another if it's needed.

For instance, let's take the toughest conversation partners of all: school-age kids. They make it so difficult to have a conversation; it's almost an oxymoron to consider kids conversation partners. Nonetheless, because they are kids, I give them the benefit of the doubt and hone my skills with my own two kids. I know I haven't lost my edge when I get them engaged in a meaningful dialogue!

My kids come through the door at the end of the day, and I ask, *How was your day at school?* In stereo, I get back, *Fine.* Instead of considering that a dead end, I follow up with another question. I inquire, *What did you like about it today?* My 16-year-old son usually says, *I don't know.* I look him right in the eye and tell him, *Really, tell me about one class you liked today.* He thinks about it for a minute. Finally he says, *Science.* And I inquire, *What did you like about science?* He launches into a colorful description of an experiment they did, and we're talking. The bottom line is that you have to open it up, and you have to show you truly care.

Digging deeper

Every Monday in offices across the country people ask each other, *How was your weekend?* That question most often nets a one-sentence reply akin to, *Good. How about yours?* Before a reply is even uttered, you are ten steps down the hall. What's the message? That you really weren't interested, you were just saying hello. *How was your vacation? How was your holiday? How's work? How are you? What's been going on? How have you been?* are just a few other ways of saying hello. It's almost universally understood that these questions are a form of greeting, not a sincere inquiry.

Most of the time the conversation ends immediately after a brief exchange. I ask my husband, Steve, *How was your day?* He replies, *Great.* The conversation evaporates — not because there was no place to go with it but because of a lack of followup. My husband doesn't think I really care about his day unless I ask more. I invite conversation by saying: *What made it so great? What went on for you today?*

Whenever you begin a dialogue with a question, be ready to dig deeper so that the other person knows you are interested in hearing more. Here are some ways to do so:

- **How was your summer?** *Excellent.* **What special things did you do?**

- **How were your holidays?** *Pretty good.* **How did you celebrate?**

- **How was your weekend?** *Good.* **What did you do?** *I went to see that new play down at the Civic Center.* **Really? You're interested in _____? I never knew that. Tell me more about that.**

- **Did you do anything relaxing?**

- **Is that something you usually do on the weekend?**

With the right queries, a conversation with a co-worker about the weekend can occupy an entire cup of coffee. The key is to have a genuine interest in what the other person is saying, along with a genuine desire to hear the response. So while you get to be quiet, you do not get to be passive. You must actively participate in the conversation.

Suppose, however, you call a customer or your boss, and the conversation is as follows when you ask about the weekend:

How was your weekend? Great. *Tell me about it.* Well, we spent some time working in the garden and that was about it. Now about this proposal.

You should recognize that the other person has steered the conversation back to business. That's the signal that the person does not want to chat at the moment. Respect those wishes by switching into a business mode.

Here are some other examples of digging deeper into a conversation: You ask, *How have you been?* and get the reply, *Busy.* Responses could include: *How do you deal with being busy? What is going on that's got you so busy? Describe a busy day for you. Do you like being busy? Does there seem to be a cycle of busy-ness during your year? Do you remember a time in your life when you weren't as busy?*

Or you ask, *Isn't this weather terrible?* and receive the reply, *It sure is.* You might respond with these: *How terrible does it get in this part of the country? What is your idea of an ideal climate? How does bad weather affect you? Have you lived anywhere else with terrible weather? What brought you here?*

Of course it's much easier to ask appropriate open-ended questions of people you know than those you are just meeting. Use discretion when meeting new people: Asking a difficult question could put the other person in an awkward position. Likewise, sometimes when we are asking open-ended questions, we really are asking questions that require only a word or two to answer. Here are some new ways to ask old favorites:

Instead of asking:	Try this:
Are you married?	**Tell me about your family.**
What do you do for a living?	**Tell me about your business/work.**
Do you have kids?	**Tell me about your family.**
What's your favorite hobby?	**Tell me about your favorite hobby.**
How was your weekend?	**What was the best part of your weekend? What went on for you this weekend?**

When you need to mingle at an industry function or take a client to lunch, prepare yourself for the event by selecting some business-related questions to ask. Here are some that work every time. Of course the goal is not to ask every one of these but to have some ready so that you feel prepared, poised, and confident.

Fail-safe Questions
for Every Business Function

- How did you get started in your business?
- How did you come up with this idea?
- What got you interested in _____ (business function, job, industry)?
- What happened first?
- Tell me what you enjoy most about your profession.
- What separates your firm from the competition?
- Describe some of the challenges of your profession.
- What will be the coming trends in your business?
- What ways have you found to be the most effective in promoting your business?
- Tell me about your most important work experience.
- What advice would you give someone just starting out in your business?
- What one thing would you do if you knew for sure that you couldn't fail?
- What significant changes have you seen since you started in your field?
- What is the most bizarre incident that you've ever experienced in your business?
- How has the Internet impacted your business? What about your profession as a whole?

Free for the taking

If you are an astute observer, you'll discover that your small-talking cohort is giving you a wealth of free information you can use to keep a conversation going. Sources of free information include:

Answers to open-ended questions. When you invite someone to tell you about his family or her job, you will receive additional free information that you can use to further the conversation. Suppose that you ask me, *Debra, how is it that you worked in product planning for AT&T?* and I say, *I was in R&D in Buffalo, New York, where I'm from, and I hated it. I hated being an engineer — they don't even make pocket protectors for women! So, I asked to be transferred anywhere. They brought me to Denver to work in product planning.* I offered lots of free information: I'm from Buffalo, I was in R&D, and I hated being an engineer. You can choose any of that free information to find more about what interests you the most. You could facilitate the conversation by asking any one of a dozen questions, including:

- *Are the winters in Buffalo really as bad as they say?*
- *Why didn't you like being an engineer?*
- *Would it have made a difference in your career if there had been pocket protectors for women?*
- *What is it like to do R&D for a corporation like AT&T?*
- *Was it tough living with a perennial Super Bowl loser?*

Appearances. Lapel pins and jewelry: The man behind me in line at the bakery was wearing a lapel pin on his suit. I asked him about it and found out that he's in the local Rotary Club. From that inauspicious beginning we had a great conversation. I shared with him that I was a Rotarian, as well.

Team apparel and other logo-identified clothing, accessories, water bottles, and clipboards are great conversation starters. Some options: *It looks like you might be a fan of the Denver Broncos. What do you think of their season?* or *I notice that you're wearing a shirt from the London Hard Rock Café. Have you been there? What did you think of it?* or *I see that you ran the "Race for the Cure," what other races have you run?*

Office and home decorations are small talk waiting to happen. A diploma on the wall gives you an opening: *What made you choose the University of Michigan for your graduate work?* And virtually any object or photograph on display is a conversation starter: *You must love golf — tell me about this trophy,* or *What an interesting piece of art. Tell me about it,* or *Tell me about this picture. Who is that with you?*

Location, location, location and occasion, occasion, occasion. The location and occasion of an event offer a wide variety of free information. At a wedding: *I was the bride's college roommate. How do you know the couple?* At a seminar or convention, simply asking, *What brought you to this event?* is an easy and unobtrusive way to start a conversation.

As I took leave of a seminar I had taught, I held the elevator for a man coming down the hall. I usually don't small talk on elevators because of the limited time; but on a whim I used the free information I had, which was that I knew there were two classrooms on that floor. Since the man had not been in my class, it was a pretty good guess that he'd come from the other. I asked him, *Were you here for a class?* He told me he'd attended a book-writing class. It turns out that I was speaking with Harry MacLean, best-selling author and teacher of the course. We continued our conversation outside of the elevator, and I now have a new friend. He even agreed to speak to my book club about his most recent book, *Once Upon a Time.* One of the reasons I love small talk is that you just never know who you'll meet or where it'll lead.

Behavior. If you are observant, you'll get a lot of free information from people's behavior. The way they speak and write can offer you small-talk starters. Notice if they are left-handed. You can inquire, *Is it challenging being left-handed? What pet peeves do you have about it?* Does the person have an accent? If so, you might say, *I thought I heard an accent. What part of the country/world are you from?* or *What brought you here?* or *What do you miss the most about where you are from?* or *What do you enjoy about your new home?*

I entered my local FedEx office with efficiency in mind — after all, that's why I'm there: I want to get in and get out. The very fact that I require the services of Fed Ex is free information that I'm in a hurry. I've got a pressing delivery. However, as I watched the clerk complete the forms, I was struck by the beautiful handwriting of this left-handed woman. I complimented her with a statement — not a question. Unfortunately, she responded as though it were an inquiry. I got the whole story of how she used to be a teacher and had purposefully perfected her handwriting… she moved to Arizona…got divorced…remarried and moved to Colorado. I could not get her to understand that I was in a hurry. She was still talking as I backed out of the door!

Fake it till you make it

Now that you are becoming small-talk savvy, practice the fundamentals. Can you recall five sure-fire questions to use in a business setting? Can you name half a dozen sources of free information? Scout your current location right now: What do you see that would make good conversation material?

You'll become skilled at small talk the same way you've improved in other activities: By practicing. It's not difficult — high-school geometry was much harder than this. All you need to do is practice. Little by little, you'll give your conversation partner plenty to talk about!

Hearing Aids and Listening Devices

We've covered half the requirements for carrying on a good conversation: how to take the lead, break the ice, and maintain a conversation. You know what works and what doesn't. However, none of this guarantees success just yet. A great conversation hinges on two things — the talking and the listening. Scientific research has shown that people are capable of listening to approximately 300 words per minute. On the flip side, most of us can only speak at 150-200 words per minute — unless you're one of those folks rattling off the disclaimer at the end of a radio spot advertising a new-car lease!

The dilemma is that we have the capacity to take in much more information than one person can divulge at any given time. So what do we do with this excess capacity? Why, we put it to use, of course. We eavesdrop on other conversations; we start thinking about what to have for dinner; we drift away into our private thoughts — and suddenly we've drifted too far...and missed something important!

Listening?

Psychologist Carl Rogers once said, "The biggest block to personal conversation is one man's inability to listen intelligently, understandingly, and skillfully to another person." Psychoanalyst Dr. Ann Appelbaum understood the source of her livelihood when she wrote in The Menninger Clinic's newsletter *Perspective,* "The image of the voice crying in the wilderness epitomizes the loneliness, the madness of not being heard. So great is our need and hunger for validation that good listeners are prized. Psychoanalysts, for example, earn a living by listening and providing responses that validate the other person."

Have you ever gone out to lunch with someone who really needs to talk? You hardly say a word. You offer support, a few kind words, a nod of the head, and you listen. The other person feels much better afterward and is ever so grateful for the conversation.

In our technology-driven world the bombarment of constant stimuli and white noise makes it a challenge to listen. Listening is no longer taken for granted. In fact, it's frequently the exception. Attentive listening has three parts: Visual, verbal, and mental. Combine these elements, and powerful listening results.

Listening is seen, not just heard

The physiological process of listening is invisible to the observer. We cannot watch the sound vibrations go into someone's ears to confirm that they received the intended message. Consequently, the speaker is always on the lookout for cues to validate receipt of the message. Visual clues, which offer the easiest form of feedback, let the speaker know you are paying attention. Facial expressions, head nods, and positive body language are clear ways of expressing interest in your conversational partner's words.

Eight-year-old Nicholas came home from school, bounded into the house, and started telling his Dad about his great day at school. "Dad," Nick said, "I had a great day at school. We had art class today, and I painted a cool picture of the mountains. We played soccer during gym and I scored a goal. And guess what — they served pizza for lunch!" Nicholas looks at his Dad reading the newspaper and sighs, "Dad, you're not listening to me!" His Dad looks up and says, "Yes I am son. You painted a picture of the mountains, you scored a goal in the soccer game, and you had pizza for lunch." Nicholas, unappeased, replies, "No Dad. That's not it. You're not listening to me with your eyes."

Even though Nick's Dad clearly heard his son, Nick felt minimized because he did not have his Dad's full attention. He wanted more than a download of facts about his day to his Dad. He wanted to see his Dad's response. He wanted to feel connected. He wanted his Dad to be invested in the story. He wanted validation while he was telling his story.

Listening is more than just hearing. It's a level of involvement that goes beyond reciting the contents of the conversation. Ray Birdwhistle, a pioneer in nonverbal communication, estimated that in a normal two-person conversation, verbal components carry less than 35 percent of the social meaning of the situation, while nonverbal components account for over 65 percent. It's critical to maintain eye contact when you are listening to another person. Don't look around at what others are doing — stay focused on the conversation at hand.

Body language also gives the speaker clues about you and your listening. The following illustration demonstrates negative and positive body language. When you cross your arms and legs, you are exhibiting defensiveness — even if your reason is cold weather! If you keep your head down and avoid eye contact, you send a message that you are avoiding interaction — even if your reason is shyness and you actually want someone to talk to you! People generally respond to these signals by ignoring you; you are not considered approachable. If you rest your chin in your hand, it appears that you are bored. Likewise, when you place your hands on your hips, you appear aggressive and unhappy with your conversation partner, or with the words you are hearing.

Engaging/Approachable Body Language

Openness vs.
Defensiveness

Expectancy vs.
Frustration

Evaluation vs.
Suspicion

Self Control vs.
Nervousness

Readiness vs.
Boredom

Confidence vs.
Insecurity

There are just as many ways to signal your interest and enthusiasm for the dialogue. You give positive messages to the speaker when you:

- **Lean forward**

- **Maintain eye contact**

- **Open up your arms and body**

- **Relax your body posture**

- **Face your partner**

- **Nod and smile**

Unlike other small-talking tricks that are easier than they look, these can be harder. It requires practice and concentration to overcome nervous habits and use positive body language. Stick with it; practice will become easier every time.

You can also increase the comfort level of your conversation partner by modifying your own style to be more similar to his. If you are chatting with someone who speaks slowly and softly, try to keep your volume down also. You can overwhelm a slow-talking, soft-spoken person with your own volume and speed. This is not to say you shouldn't be yourself; you should. However, as the "host," you want to enhance the comfort of your guest.

Verbalize your listening

Verbal cues complement the visual feedback you give a speaker. The absence of verbal cues makes a speaker wonder if anyone is listening. I called my dad, who lives in Buffalo. I was telling him a story about the kids, and there was silence on the other end of the phone. I abruptly stopped the story and asked, "Dad, are you there?" He became indignant and said, "Of course I'm here. I'm listening to you. Tell me about my grandkids." I replied, "You weren't saying anything so I though maybe you'd suddenly been buried by eight feet of snow." "I didn't want to interrupt," he replied.

There are numerous verbal cues to let the speaker know you are fully engaged in the conversation. These brief comments tell the speaker that you are interested and want to know more. You can use verbal cues to show that you have a positive response, that you disagree, or that you want to hear more about something in particular. Check out this list to see which cues are used in different situations:

If you want to show that you are:	*Say:*
Interested in hearing more...	*Tell me more. What was that like for you?*
Taking it all in...	*Hmmm, I see...*
Responding positively...	*How interesting! What an accomplishment!*
Diverging...	*On the other hand, what do you think...?*
Expanding on the idea...	*Along that same line, do you...? Why?*
Arguing/refuting...	*What proof do you have of that?*
Involving yourself...	*Could I do that? What would it mean to me?*

Clarifying...	*I'm not sure I'm clear on your feelings about...*
Empathizing...	*That must have been tough/frustrating, etc.*
Probing...	*What do you mean by that? How were you able to manage?*
Seeking specifics...	*Can you give me an example?*
Seeking generalities...	*What's the big picture here?*
Looking to the future...	*What do you think will happen next?*
Reviewing the past...	*What happened first?*
Seeking likenesses/ differences	*Have you ever seen anything like this? What's the opposing point of view?*
Seeking extremes/ contrasts	*What's the downside? What's the optimum?*

Other verbal listening cues function to redirect the conversation by transitioning to another topic. Examples of cues that offer a seamless segue include:

- That reminds me of...

- When you were talking about _____, I remembered...

- You know, I was just reading in the paper about...

- I've always wanted to ask you...

- I thought of you when I heard...

- Do you mind if I change the subject?

- There's something I've wanted to ask of someone with your expertise.

All of the above verbal cues indicate that you are fully present. Just as important, these cues encourage others to continue speaking. Imagine someone asks you a question, and you respond with a one-sentence answer. You are uncertain as to how much information they are truly interested in learning. Added verbal cues, as you respond, assure the speaker that your interest is sincere. Verbal cues encourage others to continue. Use verbal cues as an active way to get others to do the talking so that you can spend some time eating your cheeseburger!

Gabby people seldom listen. Those of us who consider ourselves quiet often congratulate ourselves for our awesome listening skills; at least we keep our mouths shut and listen! But this attitude is sometimes reflected in the lack of participation in the conversation. Too much listening and not enough verbalizing can halt a conversation, too. It is important to verbally let others know that we are following along, actively listening.

Stating the obvious

When you paraphrase what's been said, or repeat the specifics of what you have heard, there can be no doubt that

you have listened and understood the speaker. This is especially effective when you are disagreeing with your conversation partner or have listened to her explain something
highly complex or technical. Paraphrasing the speaker clari-
fies that you understood accurately. Or it can help the
speaker recognize that you misunderstood what she was
attempting to communicate. For instance: I am unhappy
with what I perceive as lack of help from my husband with
household chores. We discuss the problem. I am thrilled
when Steve promises to help more around the house. Two
weeks later I jump all over him. I am upset because I have
not witnessed his added help around the house. "You
promised to help more with household chores. When do
you plan to start keeping your promise"? I implore. "I am
helping out," Steve replies, "I've been collecting the trash
and taking it to the curb every Thursday." "That's it?" I ask. I
expected Steve to take on 50 percent of the chores. But
instead of clarifying what he meant by agreeing to my
request for help, I assumed I knew what he meant. He
assumed I meant any help would be appreciated. Men and
women will say exactly the same words and yet mean two
entirely different things. Clarify or paraphrase to prevent
misunderstandings at work and at home.

In an emotionally charged situation, you gain a side benefit of defusing anger when you repeat the specifics of what
the other person stated. People naturally calm down when
they realize they've been understood. Skilled customer service managers know that by repeating what an angry customer is saying, they can reduce the level of hostility.
Remaining calm while doing so sends a message about your
own professionalism and poise.

Before expressing apologies, before solving a problem,
let the person know that they have been heard by repeating
the specifics.

10 Tips for Tip-Top Listening

1. Learn to want to listen. You must have the desire, interest, concentration, and self-discipline.

2. To be a good listener, give verbal and visual cues that you are listening.

3. Anticipate excellence. We get good information more often when we expect it.

4. Become a "whole body" listener: Listen with your ears, your eyes, and your heart.

5. Take notes. They aid retention.

6. Listen now, report later. Plan to tell someone what you heard, and you will remember it better.

7. Build rapport by pacing the speaker. Approximate the speaker's gestures, facial expressions and voice patterns to create comfortable communication.

8. Control internal and external distractions.

9. Generously give the gift of listening.

10. Be present, watch the tendency to daydream. Don't drift off from conversations.

Mental listening skills

All the visual and verbal cues in the world are useless if you haven't stayed focused enough on the conversation to track it well. A good conversation partner retains what's been said. If you are too bored to stay with the conversation, exit gracefully instead of embarrassing your conversation partner by demonstrating boredom.

I had a business lunch with a woman who shall remain nameless. I told her a story about my kids and mentioned that my second and current husband is a periodontist. Several minutes later, during a pause in the conversation, she asked if I was married! Clearly, she had drifted away in the conversation.

Don't jeopardize a relationship by failing to listen. Your job as a conversation partner is to listen when the other person is speaking. This isn't optional — it's a required courtesy when conversing. If, for whatever reason, you cannot remain focused on what the speaker is saying, excuse yourself. The messages you send through visual, verbal, and mental cues let your partner know the status of the conversation. If you feel trapped in a conversation and don't know how to exit, read on. We'll take care of that dilemma, as well.

Prevent Pregnant Pauses with Preparation

E ven with icebreakers, conversation-makers, and active listening, there are still times when the conversation can grind to a halt if you're not prepared. Invariably, at any conference luncheon, at least one table of eight intelligent people ends up staring at their plates trying to figure out how to get the conversation rolling after they've "talked shop" ten minutes too long! They could have avoided extensive examination of the rice pilaf if just one person had been prepared. Yes, prepared — as in having done advance planning.

All eight knew that they would be sitting down with seven other people they didn't know. A good conversationalist plans before the event. No worries — slides, laptop presentations, and laser pointers are not required! All that is needed is a bit of forethought that can be accomplished in the car on the way to the event.

Don't let old acquaintances be forgotten

You need more than icebreakers to enjoy your time conversing with others. You need to tailor your preparation to the nature of the occasion and the people with whom you'll be talking. One of the toughest audiences — after kids — is an acquaintance you see only once in a while. You have some history together, you know a bit about each other, and you don't have a clue what's changed in the year since you last saw each other. In fact, it's good to assume that things probably have changed. Suppose you see a colleague annually at an industry function. In the past twelve months your colleague may have gotten a different job, experienced the death of a close friend or relative, gone on an extraordinary vacation, had a spiritual awakening, or gotten married or divorced. In other words, don't presume that you are picking up a conversation that was held a year ago. Without asking, *So what's new?*, a question that begs the conversation-stopping answer *Not much*, seek out what's new and keep the conversation rolling with questions like these:

With Acquaintances

- Bring me up to date on...
- What's been going on with work since I've seen you?
- What has changed in your life since we spoke last?
- How's your year been?
- What's new with the family?

Getting a history lesson

Frequently, you find yourself in an awkward silence or a pregnant pause in the conversation. It is up to you to either invigorate the conversation or allow it to grind to a slow halt. Do your part to charge up the conversation by being prepared with questions on the origin and history of those people you are with. For instance, you can inquire:

History Lessons

- How did you two meet?
- How did you get started ____ ?
- What got you interested in this area?
- When did you first know you wanted to be a ____ ?
- What brought you to Colorado?
- How do you all know each other?
- What got you interested in marketing?
- What gave you the idea for this business?
- What happened first?

Preparing for the long haul

Prepare for a conversation like you'd prepare for an interview: Both as the interviewer and the interviewee. It takes much less effort to prepare for a conversation than job interview, but the philosophy is the same. You want to have material prepared that is relevant to the event so that you can converse articulately and gracefully. I call the questions that fall into this category "interviewing questions"; they help keep the conversation humming along. As I drive into a parking lot before entering a meeting, luncheon, or any type of function, I prepare as if for an interview. I spend two minutes thinking about specific interviewing questions that apply to the person(s), event, or situation I am about to encounter. Most of us find ourselves seated across from a stranger we know nothing about; we panic and cannot think of anything to say. What an awkward moment! Think about it: When is the worst time to think of something to talk about? When there is nothing to talk about! Here are some examples of interviewing questions you can customize to fit your own personality:

Interviewing Questions

- What do you enjoy most about this season of the year?
- What got you involved in this organization/event?
- If you weren't here, what would you be doing at this very moment?
- If you could meet any one person, whom would you choose?
- Tell me about an issue that matters a great deal to you.
- What has been your most important work experience?

Interviewing Questions

- What word would you say describes you best?
- Do you have a personal motto or creed?
- Do you have any heroes that you greatly admire?
- What did people in high school think you were like?
- What do you do that you wish you could stop doing?

When you are getting together with a person you have spent time with before, review some of the particulars you learned on previous occasions. Maybe you discussed the MBA they were working on, or the volleyball league they coach each spring, or the fact that gardening is a beloved hobby. Don't expect to recall these specifics during a pregnant pause. Instead prepare yourself!

The nonverbal part of the conversation

One of my favorite exercises when teaching SmallTalk seminars illustrates the point beautifully. I get 10 to 12 people in a circle and arbitrarily hand one of them a ball of yarn. That person must hold onto the end of the yarn, disclose something about herself, and toss the ball of yarn to someone else in the group. The recipient must ask a question of the thrower about what she said. The recipient must then tell something about himself, hold onto the string, and toss the ball of yarn to the next person. This continues until every person has had the ball.

I love this exercise because the participants discover several things. First, since they don't know when they'll receive the ball, they pay attention to what everyone else says. Paying attention is the only way they'll be able to ask an intelligent question. Second, they learn to focus on asking *appropriate, related questions or making appropriate, related verbal cues*. Asking appropriate questions and making appropriate comments is one of the easiest ways to keep the conversation chugging seamlessly along. Lastly, they pay attention to body language, because the speaker always makes eye contact prior to throwing, so that the ball won't be dropped! If the speaker doesn't make eye contact or the listener isn't paying attention, the conversation abruptly ends with a noticeable thud.

Advance planning helps ensure that the ball doesn't get dropped. If you are at an event where you'll spend a considerable amount of time with the same group, such as a luncheon, be prepared to move beyond icebreakers and initial conversation-makers. You need to be prepared to engage in longer conversations, so you need more topics. This needn't be difficult. If you are worried that you'll forget, keep a cheat sheet in your wallet or purse to peruse just prior to lunch.

The one topic that you needn't have a list for is the one you know best: Yourself. Out of courtesy to the introverts in the crowd, I have waited until we were well into the book before getting to this point. Regardless of how many appropriate questions you have on hand, sooner or later you must talk about yourself. The rules of good conversation require give and take. If you only ask questions, your conversation partner will resent the lack of parity. It's important that each person tell about herself. This is a stretch for some people, though. It used to be a stretch for me, too. I have discovered that most people who are reticent to talk about themselves fear one or both of the following:

1. **They worry that their lives are too ordinary to be interesting.**
2. **They do not want to appear self-centered or conceited.**

Ordinary people

Guess what? Most of us are ordinary people just trying to live our lives. We worry about paying bills, educating kids, our favorite team winning a championship, getting a promotion, caring for elderly parents, taking an occasional vacation, having time for a hobby, and relaxing now and then. We are more alike than we are different, and our commonality as human beings opens the door for connection and conversation. Even ordinary people have extraordinary things happen to them that make for excellent conversation. Every person I know has had an extraordinary experience of one kind or another. Lurking somewhere in your conversation is a hilarious event, a once-in-a-lifetime vacation, a ridiculous moment, an exciting accomplishment, a hair-raising happy-ending tale, an uncanny coincidence, or an incredible adventure. Find it and bring it out! Almost anything is a conversation in the making.

Limelight etiquette

There are a few rules to remember as you reluctantly step into the limelight. You will do fine if you follow this advice — no one is skulking about with a hook looking to pull you "offstage." First, disclose information about yourself that is comfortable and uncontroversial. Lead with easy, positive, and light information. Building trust and intimacy over time creates friendships. Having a conversation is a little like peeling an onion — you want to proceed in layers, matching the level of intimacy shared by your partner.

For instance, suppose that your small-talking sidekick has just confessed that, after a long holdout, the realities of being a soccer parent caused their family to buy a minivan. This does not open the door for you to say that you've been recently diagnosed with breast cancer. However, if the conversation were taking place at "The Race for the Cure," and you were wearing a pink ribbon indicating that you were a cancer survivor, it would be acceptable to discuss breast cancer. Your choice of conversation material should be appropriate to the occasion and to the depth of rapport and intimacy established.

I recently attended a luncheon, where I was seated at one of those round tables with seven other people I had never met. We came to a lull in the conversation that instantly made everyone decide it was time to look at his or her pagers for messages. I jumped in with a story about a vacation that my family had taken over spring break. I said, *We went on a Club Med vacation in Mexico last spring and had a great time. It was so hassle-free I couldn't believe it. Since you pay a flat fee for everything, I didn't have to fish for money every time the kids wanted a Coke. They just went and got it. It seemed so effortless, and there were activities for all of us.*

My vacation story accomplished three things that rejuvenated the conversation. First, I told something about myself, giving others the opportunity to feel more connected to me. Increasing that comfort level stimulates conversation. Second, I offered a new topic that gave material for the others to use. Third, it gave my tablemates the chance to share their own experiences. Our conversation sprang to life immediately, as others jumped in with questions, stories and vacation plans of their own.

You aren't limited to talking about events and experiences. You can share feelings, opinions about books you've read, restaurants you've visited and movies you've seen. For instance, I was at an awards banquet talking with a gentleman. He said, *I'm really nervous being here. My wife had to go away on business so I'm here alone, and I don't know anyone else.* I talked with him about how nervous I used to get at social

---

Speak No Evil

Barring exceptional circumstances, avoid these often-controversial topics that can stop a conversation in its tracks:

1. Stories of questionable taste

2. Gossip

3. Personal misfortunes, particularly current ones

4. How much things cost!

5. Controversial subjects when you know where people stand

6. Health (yours or theirs). The exception is when you're talking with person who has an obvious new cast, crutches, or bandage. In that situation, the apparent temporary medical apparatus is free information. If you skirt the issue it's a bit like having an elephant in your living room and ignoring it.

functions. That brief interchange helped calm him, and we went on to converse at length about a variety of topics.

While there is an infinite list of acceptable conversation topics at public venues, there is also a short list of subjects that are generally off limits. If you are unsure about a subject's appropriateness and hesitate before bringing it up, it's probably better left unspoken. When unsure, I always invoke the old math axiom my algebra teacher taught me, *When in doubt, leave it out.* Avoid any area that is likely to offend your conversation partner.

Playing foursquare

Keeping a conversation rolling is not unlike the old playground game of foursquare. You must pass the ball among all the players and keep the ball inbounds for play to continue. This requires focusing on the ball at all times and passing it around. Some of the people in your group may be reluctant to receive the ball for the same reasons that you were — they're shy, feel like their lives are too ordinary, don't enjoy the attention, etc. It's up to you to help them, or the game will fall apart.

One of the easiest ways to start or keep a conversation going is to compliment another person. An authentic compliment makes the other person feel good about both of you, and that enhances the rapport, making conversation easier. The key is that your compliment is genuine, so select something that you can truly support. No matter what you choose, it will be one of three things: Appearance, possessions, or behavior. Mark Twain once said that a good compliment lasted him 60 days!

I had a conversation with my good friend Karen about plans for my upcoming wedding. I told her that for a period of time, I had been seeing two men — Ben and Steve. She invited me to tell her about both of them. I said, *Ben has a great sense of humor. He's the life of the party. He dresses like a million bucks and has taken me on wonderful trips. We've been to Hilton Head, Europe, and had a bunch of weekend mountain getaways. He's a great golfer and an all around wonderful guy.*

Karen could hardly contain herself, she was so excited. She said, *He sounds like a dream. I'm so happy that you're marrying him.*

I'm not, I replied. *I'm marrying Steve.*

Karen was speechless. Finally, she collected herself and said, *Well Debra, Ben sounds like a prince. Why are you marrying Steve?*

Because he makes me feel so special because of all the wonderful things he says about me. And you know what? He means every one of them!

The power in a sincere compliment is enormous. There is nothing that makes people feel more special than to have their finer traits noted and appreciated.

The perfect compliment

You can compliment someone on a new hairstyle, an item of clothing, a piece of jewelry, or physical appearance. However, not all compliments are created equal. A good compliment acknowledges the object of admiration: *That's a nice sweater you're wearing,* or *What an unusual tie.* An excellent, top-of-the-line compliment goes beyond that to give *conversation material* by expounding on why you like the item. For instance, you might elaborate on the sweater by saying, *I love your sweater. That shade really enhances the color of your eyes.* You can turn your appreciation of a good-looking tie into a more powerful compliment by saying, *That's a great tie. Its unusual design really sets it apart. I always enjoy it when men make fashion statements with their ties.*

Perhaps you are with someone who has no fashion sense whatsoever, and you have no appreciation for her taste in clothing, makeup, or accessories. Fear not — you may do better in complimenting her on a possession such as her home, an elegant fountain pen, a new car, even a coffee mug. A good compliment would be *You have a lovely home.* Turn that into state-of-the-art flattery by saying, *Your home is lovely. I really like all the photos you have — they really personalize your home and give it a lot of warmth.* Instead of saying, *This is a great cup of coffee,* consider, *I love the richness of Indonesian Sumatra, and this is a great-size mug.*

Last but not least, you can notice someone else's behavior. This is the best way to converse with kids. Instead of noticing when they do something wrong, try celebrating positive behavior. It'll go a long way toward furthering communication with them and deepening your bond. Kids aren't the only ones who appreciate compliments regarding their behavior. Adults can really open up in the wake of such acknowledgment.

I know a realtor who took a couple house-hunting one Sunday. She drove them all over town and probably showed them over 30 houses. They went in and out of neighborhoods in town, in the suburbs, the works. After six hours, they had completely run out of things to say and still hadn't found a single house that the couple was remotely considering. The realtor was tired and just about out of ideas. Then she said, *I really admire that you know exactly what you want. You're not going to settle for something that you don't want and then possibly be unhappy with your choice later.* That one compliment got the couple charged up again and they were able to find a new topic of conversation to get them through the day, although they didn't locate their dream house that Sunday.

Other behavioral compliments include comments like:

- **I appreciate how organized you are for our meetings. It makes it easy to get the work done.**

- **It must have taken a lot of courage to change careers during your peak success. I really admire that.**

- **You have an amazing amount of determination. I think it's remarkable that you set aside time to successfully train for a marathon. Congratulations.**

- **I know you are nervous about this procedure; it's great that you made yourself show up.**

- **You certainly look at the bright side of things; it is a pleasure to work with you.**

- **You manage to run such an organized home, even with four children!**

Again, the ticket to a successful pat on the back is that you offer it sincerely. You may find that the person you are complimenting has difficulty receiving the praise. He may try to neutralize the compliment by denying it or feel obligated to return a compliment. If that happens, reaffirm your sincerity and move on to another subject.

Adding FORM and substance

Besides complimenting the other person, another way to draw a reluctant speaker into the conversation is to toss her the ball by asking a question. In addition to the icebreakers back in Chapter Two, there are four categories of questions that are effective in social situations. I use the acronym FORM to remember them:

Family

Tell me about your family.
Does everyone live in the area?
What do you like best about being a father/mother/son/ aunt, etc.?

Occupation

What got you into your current job?
How did you come up with that idea?
What are some of the toughest challenges in your job?
If you could change one thing about your job, what would it be?
How has the Internet impacted your business/industry?

Recreation

What do you do for fitness?
What kinds of things does your family do for fun?
How do you spend your leisure time?
What's been your favorite vacation?

Miscellaneous *Have you seen any good movies lately?*
What do you think about _____ (news event)?
Are you reading anything you really enjoy?

No matter what your chosen topic of conversation, I cannot overstate the importance of being authentic when talking with someone. If you are not genuinely interested in what the other person is saying, no amount of planning or preparation will save you from a doomed conversation. Interest in someone else cannot be feigned. If you truly cannot muster any enthusiasm for the dialogue, you owe it to your partner to excuse yourself and make your way to another approachable person.

The March of progress

You are now about two-thirds of the way through this book. By now, you've become familiar with techniques to make you an excellent conversationalist. It's now a good time to reflect a on how far you've come as you practice these skills and identify the opportunities for improvement that lay before you. Look at yourself in the mirror and respond with an honest "YES" or "NO" to the following statements:

- **I'm conscious of taking turns in conversations so that I can find out about others and help them get to know me.**

- **I have joined or participated in at least one club or group activity in order to develop new business friendships.**

- **I have used my contacts to help at least two people find new jobs or hook up with potential customers and clients. I have given information to someone for other networking purposes.**

- **I go to at least two functions a month where I can meet people in my profession/industry or potential decision-makers.**

- **If another person is friendly to me, I find it easy to be friendly back. However, I wait to make sure the other person is friendly before I'm friendly in return.**

- **When someone asks, "What's new?" instead of saying, "Not much," I often talk about something exciting in my life.**

How did you do? If you're like me, you probably still have some work to do. It takes effort and practice to change habits. I suggest that you write down one statement reflecting what you want to conquer. Focus on that one goal until you feel comfortable, and then move on to the next. When you stay focused, it won't take long!

Crimes and Misdemeanors

I travel quite a bit, small talking my way across the country. One of the biggest trends I've seen is an increase in "assault on a conversation with a deadly weapon." I've been victimized myself a couple of times. You should know that these people are armed and dangerous, and if they enter your dialogue, you are at serious risk of witnessing the tortuous murder of your conversation. Stay on your toes; these people are cleverly disguised. They can orchestrate several costume changes at a single event and impersonate people in every profession. If you sense danger, stay calm. Be on the lookout for these renegades. One further cautionary note: Often, the worst offenders are staring us in the mirror.

I've decided it's time to get more aggressive in preventing conversational crimes. I've done an extensive investigation on this phenomenon and have organized the killers into eight classifications. During the course of your own daily conversation, try not to add your own name to the "Conversational Criminals Most Wanted" list. Here are some crime-fighting techniques to keep honest conversationalists safe.

The FBI agent

1. The FBI agent

The FBI agent definitely does not have the national interest at heart. He or she can be seen stalking casual conversations and pulling people aside for interrogation. You will immediately recognize their unmistakable modus operandi, because they fire question after question at you, like a machine gun in a jungle. *What do you do for a living? Where are you from? You married? Got any kids? Lived here long? How long have you been on the job? What's your mother's maiden name?*

Notice that the FBI agent relentlessly assaults his captive with a barrage of questions. He leaves no opportunity for his captive to offer a confession of any kind. The captive is not allowed to expand, offer additional evidence, ask questions, or even have a glass of water. Forget about making a phone call or getting a lawyer. The captive is forced to give staccato answers just to keep pace. He is held in custody at the whim of the interrogator, who, when finished with the questioning, unceremoniously dumps the captive and moves on to round up another suspect.

The interrogatory method seldom works to anyone's satisfaction. The agent would be much more successful if he asked open-ended questions requiring more extensive answers. The detainee would cough up plenty of information effortlessly if given the opportunity. The agent also makes the mistake of settling for one- or two-word answers, when digging deeper could have uncovered motives, alibis, opportunities, and background information that would have proved quite helpful in the agent's quest for conversation had he asked appropriate, probing questions.

The FBI agent is characterized by his exceptional nervousness. Help this person out by taking control of the conversational ball. Ask him an open-ended question. Follow up — dig deeper and use verbal listening cues. For instance, ask what he does for a living. Follow up with questions about what that kind of job entails and how he got into it. Become the host and attend to his comfort. This will allow you to slow down the conversation. Eventually you'll ease into a nice rhythm, a back-and-forth volley with the conversational ball.

2. The braggart

This convict made his way onto The Most Wanted List by executing a series of conversational mass murders in almost every state. He frequently appears during periods of self-disclosure. He will boast of his accomplishments, embellish the truth, and brag about feats mighty and small in a very self-aggrandizing manner. He usually makes no attempt to go incognito, so arrogant is he. His goal is to gain status in the eyes of those in attendance, so he welcomes an audience. The bigger the group, the more bravado he feels. He has been known to kill multiple conversations with a single appearance.

His trademark is that he will always relate all of his accomplishments. He made a killing on the stock market. He'll tell how he outwitted the financial experts by choosing a long shot that paid off big. Of course his son is the captain of the baseball team, and pro scouts are recruiting the boy. He'll spare you no details. Perhaps he just bought a top-of-the-line gizmo. He can't imagine why everyone else doesn't do the same. He always has an "I'm king of the world" story to tell.

The braggart's sister, Braggarta, is equally lethal, although she prefers single encounters with people she knows. She usually prefers to do her boasting in a more personal way. She tends to speak conspiratorially to members of her inner circle. She leaves it to them to spread the word of her greatness to unknown parties. Braggarta never directly discloses her greatness to strangers. She lets them find out from her coterie of confidantes who are charged with telling others. While strangers are not required to bow to Braggarta, it is expected that they will be suitably impressed.

She will very quietly tell her inner circle about her new designer kitchen and how much it cost. She'll tell them about a smashing vacation on the French Riviera that everyone else must take. In fact, she'll give you the name of her travel agent just so you can replicate the trip.

The only hope of stopping a small talk murder orchestrated by the braggart is to bring the conversation back to more general topics, such as current events. You can also refocus the conversation on your own life, telling about something that you are currently doing. There is no point in going toe-to-toe with either of them, because it is impossible to directly stave off their boastfulness. Your only weapon is redirecting the conversation.

3. Can you top this? (the one-upper)

Members of this longstanding conversational crime family are first cousins to the braggart and his sister. These folks generally come from a patriarchal lineage, as women have a slightly different method to their murder. While the one-uppers generally do not brag first, they always top someone else's story. They seem to be completely unaware that they have offended other small talkers by constantly trumping another person's story. Sometimes the one-uppers genuinely believe they are showing compassion and demonstrating excellent listening skills by topping another's tale.

You know the scene. Your colleague Brian is looking for a new job, and you inquire about how the search is progressing. As soon as Brian offers an update, John launches into a tale about his own difficulties on the job, making it seem like unemployment is preferable to his own job woes.

Before you know it, the group is talking all about what's going on in the industry, and Brian's job search is lost in the shuffle. His troubles aren't acknowledged. No solutions are offered. No sympathy is given. No encouraging words found him. Brian is left feeling like no one really cares about his plight. While John might have thought he was being supportive, he wasn't. He simply diverted attention away from Brian and onto himself.

Women are also experts at topping another's story, but their approach is to match someone else's. For instance, Rose talks about relationship problems she's having with Steven, and Shelley commiserates by saying, *Honey, I know just what you mean. My Anthony had the nerve to....*The woman who topped the initial woman's story didn't really commiserate. She stole the show. She took the spotlight off the other woman and put it right on herself. She stopped the other woman in the middle of her story.

A particularly troublesome spot for women is talking about their kids. Sometimes I have to fight myself from jumping in and telling my own kid tales when another woman is telling a story about hers. Instead of enjoying the story she is sharing, I can get sidetracked, because her story reminds me of something similar that my kids did at that age. I get so excited that I just want to jump right in there because I'm exhilarated by the conversation. This is not a stalled conversation – this is one in which everyone wants the ball! However, it's very deflating to the person telling the original story. Her story is the one that got the group so enthusiastic. It's important to acknowledge that and to enjoy such a great story. There's no need to rush to the next. It's like hurrying through a glass of fine wine – you miss most of the experience in the rush to complete it!

Be aware of one of the most prevalent "one-upping" statements circulating these days: *Been there, done that.* In one very short sentence, the person uttering those four words is saying that the story is old news, that there is nothing else to say about that topic. It lets the other person know, in no uncertain terms, that his experience is universal and he can spare the rest of us the details of such a boring story. Crime stoppers report that it is tough to topple the one-upper, who is quite successful in crushing the conversation to death. Those still standing usually attempt to regroup in a clandestine fashion to prevent another crime.

4. The monopolizer

A master of disguise, the monopolizer has managed to infiltrate conversations across the country. Victims are shocked to discover that even a very introverted and shy person can turn out to be a monopolizer. The monopolizer can turn up anywhere, even at the most exclusive of events. They strike boldly, seizing the conversation in plain view of all. They can enter any conversation and artfully gain control before a single person can react. There is never any shortage of witnesses to the monopolizer's crimes; nevertheless, people are initially too captivated to take action. The monopolizer takes the spotlight through self-disclosure and retains it by continuing to "peel the layers of the onion" without regard to whether anyone in the group is feeling any discomfort.

Monopolizers feel justified: They believe they are performing a community service by keeping the conversational ball rolling. Usually shy people who find that the spotlight is rather fun can be the worst offenders. Instead of hogging the ball, the monopolizer should pass it to someone else in the group. I have a personal rule that I never talk for more than five minutes before passing the ball. Time can fly when we are talking about ourselves! No matter what the topic — how I lost 65 pounds, how I got into business, why my kids are so incredible — the clock is ticking. When my five minutes are up, I pass the ball to someone else with an appropriate question or comment. It's not just our golfing buddies or in-laws who are monopolizers!

If you are alone with a monopolizer, you have several options to salvage the situation. If you are with your boss, a client, or your mother-in-law, it's usually best to surrender and give the gift of listening. Once in a while you can be successful for brief interludes by changing the topic, using self-disclosure, or asking a prepared question. However, it is impossible to make a monopolizer stop. You can't change another person. If your career or your relationship with your extended family is on the line, just surrender and consider it a random act of kindness.

There are occasions when you can successfully stop a monopolizer. When you are approaching your saturation point, throw out a white flag as a warning. Just like a racecar driver gets a white flag indicating time constraints, you must throw one before you can legitimately stop a monopolizer in his tracks. For example: You are in your office, and your friend Gary comes by to tell you about his golf game. When you are running out of time, interest, or willpower, you throw a white flag by saying, *Wow, Gary. That's an amazing round you shot. Before you continue, I need to let you know that in a few minutes I have to get back to preparing the budget.* You have politely given Gary the signal that you need to end the conversation shortly. Gary takes another four minutes telling you of his exploits on the 12th and 13th holes. You can now wrap it up by saying, *Well, Gary, that's really something. I have to take care of the budget right now. Maybe we can catch up another time.* You can now turn your attention to your budget without worry. You were gracious and obliging, and you gave fair warning that it was time to end the chat.

If you are in a group of three or more, assume the role of

host and make an interception. Every year I get together to catch up with some college friends for an evening. My friend Lori is infamous for her legendary ability to monopolize the conversation. Given my line of work, I feel it obligated to help the group and facilitate passing the ball. So I jump in after she's had more than her five minutes on the floor and say, *Lori, that's a great story about Adam's hitting streak. Marilyn, what's been going on with your kids?* Connecting Lori's story about her son to Marilyn's kids lends continuity to the conversation while diplomatically allowing someone else a chance to talk. As Uncle Joe is going on endlessly about the life of an auditor, transition the conversation to someone else. *That sounds tough, Uncle Joe. Cousin Larry, what's going on for you at work?*

Monopolizers have shown that they are candidates for rehabilitation. They have been successful in restoring conversational balance once they realize that talking incessantly is not exactly a favor to everyone else. Remember that as the host, your goal is not only to get the monopolizer to yield the floor, it is to include others — especially the quiet ones. Invite them into the dialogue with a question or comment directed to them. Even when there isn't a monopolizer in the conversation, pass the ball to everyone.

5. The interrupter

Beware the interrupter! This villain comes in all shapes, sizes, and haircuts. I've often wondered if the interrupter was prevented from ever finishing a sentence as a kid and is retaliating against society. The interrupter is characterized by high drive, determination to make her point, and a lack of patience. I confess that I have done time as an interrupter. I was convicted for interrupting my husband relentlessly. I was on probation for a while, but after three strikes, I was in the joint. My husband is very low-key, and my conviction caused him a great deal of angst. He understood my temperament and was torn about confronting me. But after I interrupted him one too many times, he demanded relief.

Frequently, he would start to say something and provide rationale for his point. If I didn't agree, I'd jump right in without letting him finish. I didn't want to wait three minutes for him to finish his point. It was an eternity. Most interrupters are like me. We interrupt because we think we know what you're going to say, so let's not waste time. Or we know that you are wrong, and we must hurry to point out the errors in your thinking.

However, having already gone through one divorce, I wasn't interested in destroying our near-perfect union with my short attention span and lack of patience. I have since realized that interruptions badly sabotage a good conversation, so now I campaign against them. There are only two good reasons for interrupting. The first is that you need to exit immediately. The second is that the topic of conversation is too uncomfortable to bear, and you need to change the subject right away.

6. The poor sport

The poor sport has an unparalleled reputation for small-talk suicide. The poor sport will kill her own conversation by refusing to play by the rules. A very cunning illusion artist, the poor sport changes open-ended questions into closed-end quips. Using smoke and mirrors, the poor sport always finds a way to reduce a beautiful question into a simple one-word answer. When asked, *What did you do this weekend?* the poor sport will reply with, *Nothing.* The question left plenty of room for the poor sport to select some aspect of the weekend for conversation. Instead, she starved the conversation by withholding food. The poor sport just doesn't play well with others. She ignores the rules, pouts as it suits her, and quits the game without warning.

Some poor sports simply have never been properly trained; they don't know how to ask open-ended questions themselves. With an outreach program, some of them show promise. You can help out a poor sport by answering a closed-ended question as if it had been open-ended. For instance, if a poor sport asks, *How was your weekend?* don't just say, *Great. What about yours?* Instead, teach by example. Offer, *Great. We took the kids skiing and it was perfect day. The only glitch was that Mike took a bad spill, but he's okay now.* You have helped out the poor sport because you've given her lots of material with which she can ask a related question to keep the conversation from a reaching a quick demise. You've offered information about yourself that can help bridge distance and create conversation. One cautionary note: It is very easy to become the monopolizer in the presence of a poor sport. Exercise restraint and keep tossing the ball back to the other person. Offer information that will contribute to the conversation, but don't steal the show!

7. The know-it-all

These nasty criminals will mow you down with arrogance and condescension. They know everything, and they tell you so. They just knew that the stock market was going to take a dive or hit a high. In fact, they knew that the election would be close, that the winter was going to be brutal, etc., etc., etc. There just is no end to what they know. Since they know that they are always right, they see no point in soliciting other opinions. They cut them down without compunction. In seconds they can silence an entire group because no one wants to risk humiliation at the hands of the-know-it-all. Watch out for the person who has absolute-ly no interest in anyone else's opinions but his own.

Be careful if you flaunt your opinions. Make sure that others realize you are only offering your personal opinion about what works for you. There is one simple question that, when used properly, prevents anyone from becoming a know-it-all. It is this four-word query: *What is your opinion?*

8. The advisor

The advisor always leaves her calling card at the scene of the crime. She is readily identifiable by her endless array of solutions to everyone else's problems. She's a veritable Ann Landers, Ms. Manners, Oracle at Delphi, and Dr. Ruth rolled into one. There is nothing she can't solve — even when you don't want solutions! She generously offers unsolicited advice without charge.

Despite her generous nature, the advisor is a true outlaw. She decimates a perfectly good chat by meddling. The truth is, most people don't want advice — they want empathy and compassion. When the advisor rides in on her white horse to save the day, she minimizes the very person she's trying to rescue. She presumes that in hearing a tiny snippet of anoth-er's dilemma, she has an intimate understanding of the prob-lem and knows the perfect solution. The advisor would do much better digging deeper to learn more about the issue and offering support instead of unsolicited solutions.

The advisor is very seductive because she is upbeat, con-fident, and wants to help. That's what makes her so wily. It is easy to unwittingly emulate her. In fact, I just did my impersonation of the advisor and was mortified once I real-ized it! I was having lunch with my friend Bill who recently received a promotion to manager of a large sales territory for a medical supply company. He was talking about the difficulties with a new sales rep: the guy's sales were off, he wasn't making headway, he was discouraged, etc. Well, I just chimed right in with all the solutions for him. I said, *I think the key to success is sell, sell, sell. Visibility is everything. I just kept knocking on doors till they started opening.*

Bill didn't need my advice; he needed my support. He just wanted to talk about his difficulties and share his thoughts. In giving solutions, I wasn't empathic. I was presumptuous. Bill did not ask for advice. He wasn't seeking my infinite wisdom — he wanted an attentive ear. Don't make the same mistake. Give the gift of listening and offer advice only when it's solicited.

Advisors are everywhere. I had an encounter with one on the ski slopes of Colorado. I was in Vail to teach a SmallTalk seminar to ski instructors. I decided to ignore my fear of heights and take a ski lesson to better see how the instructors might best use small talk. I was grouped with a family from Alabama who had never even seen snow before. As the lesson progressed, the instructor noticed how cautiously I was skiing — I was even more reticent than the Alabamians! The instructor decided that I must have had weak quad muscles. He showed me some strengthening exercises to solve that problem.

The real problem was that the advisor/instructor diagnosed the difficulty without even consulting me. He had no idea that I am an avid runner; my quad strength is fine, thank you very much! My terror at standing at an altitude of over 11,000 feet practically paralyzed me. Had the instructor bothered to find that out, he would have given me a much more effective skiing lesson. Had he dug deeper, he would have discovered that his premature analysis of my problem was completely incorrect.

Physicians are among the most notorious advisors. They frequently interrupt the patient and diagnose the problem before the patient has a chance to tell the whole story. Frequently, the patient doesn't get to the heart of the matter until the doctor has his hand on the doorknob, about to exit the room. If the doctor would sit and listen to the patient completely before rendering an opinion, the appointment would be much more successful. Each would enjoy reduced frustration and a better outcome!

A crime-free conversation

These eight criminals can bleed the life right out of any conversation. Sure, there are criminal lookalikes, too. Most of those folks are petty criminals specializing in misdemeanors that can hurt a good gab session but can't kill it. You have the skills to deal with these kinds of infractions. However, when you recognize one of "The Most Wanted," exercise extreme caution. Even the most vigilant conversationalist can still get ambushed. You can even take down your own conversation, because the truth is, we each have a rap sheet. I'm a chronic interrupter when I don't police myself. Chances are that unless you are impersonating Mother Teresa, you have a conversational weakness that could land you on The Most Wanted list if you're not careful. Be on the lookout for your own criminal activity, for you may be aiding and abetting the murder of a good conversation.

Even if you take the high road and have a clean conversational record, you never know when you'll find yourself with a convicted felon on the loose slaughtering perfectly good small talk. Sometimes, there's nothing that can be done except to preserve your own safety with a quick getaway. Knowing that, it behooves you to have several escape routes planned so you can exit in a hurry if need be. Fear not — I wouldn't leave you in harm's way. Your escape hatch is waiting.

The Graceful Exit

Whether you are trying to escape a convicted conversation killer or just want to circulate more, there are ways to artfully exit a conversation that leave the other person's ego intact. I find that many people remain in a conversation longer than they should for two reasons: they feel trapped, especially if it's just a two-person dialogue, or they are so comfortable that they don't want to leave. If you are at a party or an industry meeting and your goal is to meet people, you must find the courage to leave a conversation in order to accomplish your goals. Done properly, an authentic farewell will actually enhance your relationship.

When you prepare to depart a conversation, recall why you originally connected with your conversation partner and bring the conversation back to that topic. Doing so will allow you to make a meaningful connection and then take your leave easily. For instance, I was at an open house thrown by a large corporation. Before I left my conversation partner, I said, *Tom, it's been wonderful talking with you about the changes impacting the healthcare industry. I need to catch up with another client before she leaves. Thanks for sharing your expertise.* Tom returned the compliment, we shook hands, and I headed to my client while Tom went in another direction.

Notice that I didn't make excuses for my leaving. I didn't

say I had to call the babysitter or that I needed to return a page. That well-known adage "honesty is the best policy" is really true. It's important to retain your poise and state your reason for departing courteously. Even if you despised the conversation and are chomping at the bit to leave, be tactful as you go. Here are some diplomatic ways to make your exit:

Exit Lines

- I need to go see the exhibits.

- I want to go talk to the speaker.

- I'm going to circulate and meet some of the new members.

- I want to see if there are any other people from my industry here today.

- I must speak with the membership chairperson before she leaves.

- I promised myself that I'd meet three new people before I leave this evening.

- I want to meet some other potential clients this morning.

- I want to get around and say hello to everyone at this meeting/party.

These exit lines are successful because they put the focus directly on you. You clearly state that the reason you are leaving the conversation is that *you need to do something.* There is no mistaking the fact that you have a specific agenda that you are trying to accomplish. By highlighting your own goals, you take the burden off your conversation partner. Your small-talking associate now knows that your need to move on has nothing to do with the quality of time you just spent with that person.

The cardinal rule of the exit is that when you depart, you do what you said you were going to do. If you said goodbye to Joanne by telling her that you were going to see the exhibits, go do it. If you allow yourself to get sidetracked en route to your new destination, you run the risk of insulting your former partner. For instance, if Vince stops you on your way to the exhibits, do not stay and talk! Instead, say, *Vince, it's good to see you. I was just on my way to the exhibits. Would you like to join me or can I catch up with you afterward?* If you make the mistake of getting immersed in a conversation with Vince, all Joanne sees is that you didn't go to the exhibits. She now presumes that you were never headed there, and that your true goal was just to end the conversation. You now have a tarnished reputation, an upset person, and other possible unintended consequences. Don't burn a bridge by failing to get to your next destination!

Taking care of business

Staying focused on your own agenda will make your small talking much more productive than if you are just casually mingling with whomever walks through the door. You will have questions prepared and a cast of characters in mind that you'd like to meet. Keeping track of your own progress toward accomplishing your objectives will help you gain the motivation to exit one conversation and get involved in another. It also provides you with a number of getaway lines.

You can invoke your partner's help in exiting by getting a referral or asking for business. For instance, you've been talking to Shelly for about 15 minutes and you need to see some other people before the cocktail party ends. Shelly can actually help you do that if you let her. You say, *Shelly, I've* been having trouble with the graphics package on my Mac at home. *Do you know anyone here who uses this program on a PC?* Shelly will either give you a lead to the appropriate person, or she'll say she doesn't know anyone with that program. Either way, you've created a clean break. If Shelly can't help you, you simply thank her, tell her that you really need to find someone, and say goodbye. It's just that easy. Don't invent a problem just to end a conversation. Mentally check your agenda and ask for a referral to someone connected to forwarding your goals.

Suppose that you want to find a prospective client or a new job for yourself. If you came to the party with that agenda, you need to verbalize it to accomplish it. You can do this easily without putting your conversation partner on the spot. You simply say, *Patrick, do you know anyone who might have some ideas about where I could find an engineering job?* A question such as this nets you a couple of good results. First, it lets the other party know in a very unobtrusive way that you are in the job market. Patrick just might be able to help you. The second accomplishment is that you've opened up channels with other people. Patrick may say, *I'm sorry I can't help you with that Debra, but Jim, over there by the bar, is an engineer. He probably has some ideas for you.* You can graciously leave the conversation and head over toward someone who may be able to assist you with your goal. You easily introduce yourself to Jim saying, *I was just talking with Patrick, and he told me that you're an engineer.* You have an introduction and a topic of conversation with no effort or angst. You may even get a new job out of the deal!

Don't hesitate to ask for business or referrals as you take your leave from a conversation. Every person at a business meeting has an agenda — and virtually everyone there is seeking new business. There is no shortage of ways to ask for referrals or business. Here are some methods to take care of business; try some out and tailor a couple to fit your personality:

Business: Ask for Referrals

- Can you recommend anyone who needs a _____; I'd appreciate the referral.
- Can you suggest anyone with whom I could speak about _____?
- Who do you know that might be able to help me with _____?
- I had hoped to meet someone who is interested in _____. Do you know anyone like that?
- Who else here could I speak to about joining the _____ committee?

These techniques are not unique to business situations. You can easily adapt them to social events, as well. Here are some examples:

Social: Ask for Referrals

- I'd like to find someone who's interested in hiking or who has info on hiking groups. Do you know whether anyone here can help me?
- Do you know anyone here who's also new to this area?
- I'm going to look for someone interested in volunteer activities.

The changing of the guard

A time-honored tradition of leaving a conversation is executing the changing of the guard. When a new person enters the group and begins talking to one or two people, one or more other people bow out. It is a quick and easy escape used by people all the time. The downside of this technique is that it *only* facilitates an exit, but if you are just looking for the nearest emergency exit, this is your ticket.

A slight variation on the theme is to take your conversation partner with you as you exit. This can be done even when it's just the two of you talking. You introduce your conversational party to someone who can render assistance to him. This transition is easily made with statements like these:

Ask Them to Join You

- I'd like to introduce you to an associate of mine who's in your field. Let's see if she's around.

- Matt is a great guy with an interesting history. I'd like to introduce you two.

- Let's go meet the speaker.

- I see my friend Jennifer is here. Let's go say hi.

- Let's circulate. I promised myself I'd meet some new people.

- Let's go get some dinner.

Issuing an invitation for your partner to join you on your way to another destination is a very gracious and considerate way to exit. You are still focused on your own agenda, but you haven't left your associate high and dry. Reverse the situation and think about the other person inviting you to join her. It's a perfect opportunity to get introduced to another person, or you can gracefully decline, feeling positive about the offer.

A little appreciation goes a long way

Ending a conversation by showing appreciation for the interchange provides an upbeat way to leave on a positive

Show Appreciatiom

- It was wonderful to see you and hear about the convention.
- I've really enjoyed talking with you about your new business.
- I appreciate your willingness to share your expertise.
- Thank you for the delightful conversation.
- I'm so glad you introduced me to the subject of _____. It's very interesting.
- It's nice to meet someone involved in ____.
- It was so thoughtful of you to introduce me to _____. Thanks.
- I appreciate your effort to include me in the conversation. It's tough being new, and you made it easier for me.

note. Thanking others for their time, expertise, or the sheer joy of the conversation is always welcome. You emanate poise and self-confidence when you bid adieu by expressing your gratitude and praising your partner in some way. This is accomplished in much the same way as using a compliment to forward a conversation, and the same rule applies: Be genuine. Done sincerely, offering gratitude will produce a wave of goodwill and a positive association with your name. Appreciation is a compliment with closure. You've ended the conversation on a personalized note, and both you and your partner separate feeling good about each other. Some ways to do this are shown on the previous page.

Remember to end the conversation the same way you began it — with a smile and a handshake. Even if you have to get up and walk around the table to do this, make sure you do. You make a lasting impression when you seal a conversation with a handshake. Just that fleeting hand-to-hand moment enhances the rapport you've worked hard to establish. Melting away into the crowd discredits your integrity and your intentions. The end of the conversation represents the last opportunity to establish a connection with someone. Capitalize on it with a vengeance!

Parting is such sweet sorrow

If you've met someone with whom you'd like to further a relationship, the best way to exit is to ask to see him again. Assume the burden of issuing the invitation regardless of gender. If you are female, do not think that you have to wait for the male to make the offer — whether it's a business or social engagement. I'm not in the business of dispensing singles advice so don't construe this as such. This is about using small talk successfully to accomplish your goals. If your goal was to meet a new person and cultivate a relationship, then do so. Gender is immaterial.

Muster your moxie and just do it. Sure, you'll feel a bit out of your comfort zone, but the only way to pick the fruit is to get out on a limb. Realize that if you get turned down, it's not a statement about you – the other person doesn't know you well enough to draw any conclusions about you. Remember my friend Rex…his shyness was the reason he didn't invite me to sit with him. If someone turns you down, you can't possibly know the reason unless it is offered. Here are some ways to invite the other person to continue the relationship:

Issue an Invitation

- I don't want to monopolize your time this evening. Can we arrange to meet later?

- Will I see you at the next meeting?

- I'll be thinking of you during your _____. May I call you when you get back?

- I'd enjoy spending some time with you. Can I phone you to set up a convenient time?

- I'll drop off that article we discussed at your office next week. I'll phone you and schedule a time.

- I'd like to rehash what we did in class tonight. Would you like to join me for a cup of coffee?

- I enjoyed working out with you. Do you want to meet next week and do it again?

- I hope we can do business together soon. May I call you in the coming days to determine your level of interest?

Before you leave a conversation, have a clear destination in mind. You don't necessarily need to head to another conversation. Feel free to get something to eat, get a fresh beverage, call the sitter and check on the kids, use the restroom, or even take a stroll around the room. Movement attracts attention, so make sure that you don't look lost. If your former conversation partner perceives that you're wandering around aimlessly, he's likely to feel insulted that you prefer your own company to his.

Because the manner in which you exit a conversation leaves a lasting impression, you want to develop finesse at graceful departures. There is nothing mysterious about these techniques, no rocket science required. They are common-sense tips, but they are not common practice. Practice frequently until you can comfortably disengage yourself from conversations using a variety of methods. Acquiring this skill will undoubtedly improve your overall confidence and presence. That enhanced poise will, in turn, make you an ever-more-inviting conversation partner.

The Conversational Ball is in Your Court!

50 Ways to Fuel a Conversation

Here's a cheat sheet full of tips to review before any event, occasion, interview, or date. Always take the risk and assume the burden. Check out the following, go to whatever meeting, luncheon, or party awaits and seize the day!

1. Be the first to say hello.
2. Introduce yourself to others.
3. Take risks and anticipate success.
4. Remember your sense of humor.
5. Practice different ways of starting a conversation.
6. Make an extra effort to remember people's names.

50 Ways to Fuel a Conversation

7. Ask a person's name if you've forgotten it.

8. Show curiosity and sincere interest in finding out about others.

9. Tell others about the important events in your life. Don't wait for them to draw it out.

10. Demonstrate that you are listening by restating their comments in another way.

11. Communicate enthusiasm and excitement about your subjects and life in general.

12. Go out of your way to try to meet new people wherever you are.

13. Accept a person's right to be an individual with different ideas and beliefs.

14. Let the natural in you come out when talking with others.

15. Be able to succinctly tell others — in a few short sentences — what you do.

16. Reintroduce yourself to someone who is likely to have forgotten your name.

17. Be ready to tell others something interesting or challenging about what you do.

18. Be aware of open and closed body language.

19. Smile, make eye contact, offer a handshake, and go find the approachable person.

20. Greet people that you see regularly.

21. Seek common interests, goals, and experiences with the people you meet.

22. Make an effort to help people if you can.

50 Ways to Fuel a Conversation

23. Let others play the expert.

24. Be open to answering common ritualistic questions.

25. Be enthusiastic about other people's interests.

26. See that the time is balanced between giving and receiving information.

27. Be able to speak about a variety of topics and subjects.

28. Keep up to date on current events and issues that affect our lives.

29. Be willing to express your feelings, opinions, and emotions to others.

30. Use "I" when you speak about your own feelings and personal things, rather than "you."

31. Visually show others that you are enjoying your conversation with them.

32. Be ready to issue invitations to others to join you for other events/activities to further the relationship.

33. Find ways to keep in touch with friends and acquaintances you meet.

34. Seek out others' opinions.

35. Look for the positive in those you meet.

36. Start and end your conversations with the person's name and a handshake or warm greeting.

50 Ways to Fuel a Conversation

37. Take the time to be friendly with your neighbors and co-workers.

38. Let others know that you would like to get to know them better.

39. Ask others about things that they have told you in previous conversations.

40. Listen carefully for free information.

41. Be ready to ask open-ended questions to learn more.

42. Change the topic of conversation when it has run its course.

43. Always search for the things that really get another excited.

44. Compliment others about what they are wearing, doing, or saying.

45. Encourage others to talk to you by sending out positive signals.

46. Make an effort to see and talk to people you enjoy.

47. When you tell a story, present the main point first and then add the supporting details afterward.

48. Include everyone in the group in conversation whenever possible.

49. Look for signs of boredom or lack of interest from your listener.

50. Prepare ahead of time for each social or business function.

Make the Most of Networking Events!

L earn how to make the most of meetings, interviews, and networking events or of entertaining clients at conventions, trade shows, and other work-related functions.

Do you dread receptions, banquets, and other business-related social events? Does attending another open house make you want to run inside your own and lock the door? You're not alone. Many of us are apprehensive about these situations, because most of us either hate entering rooms where we don't know anyone or hate spending time with people we don't know well. Keeping a conversation going during such occasions is an ordeal.

But for business professionals, these occasions represent opportunities to develop business friendships and broaden our networks. Whether you realize it or not, networking happens all the time.

During an awkward social gathering, demanding sales presentation, or a tough interview, small talk can turn a challenging situation into a success. Small talk connects us, whether the setting is business or social.

Networking??

Everyone learns the technical skills required for their jobs, but not everyone places importance on conversational skills. The ability to talk easily with anyone is a learned skill, not a personality trait. Acquiring it will help you develop rapport with people and leave a positive impression that lasts longer than an exchange of business cards.

Here are a few tips business professionals can use to improve their small-talk skills:

- **Be the first to say hello!**

- **Introduce yourself.** Act as if you're the host and introduce new arrivals to your conversational partner or partners.

- **Smile first and always shake hands when you meet anyone.**

- **Take your time during introductions!** Make an extra effort to remember names, and use them frequently in the conversation.

- **Maintain eye contact in any conversation.** Many people in a group of three or more people look around in the hope that others will maintain eye contact on our behalf. But people don't feel listened to if you're not looking at them.

- **Get somebody to talk** about why they're attending the event, and you are on your way to engaging them in conversation.

- **Show an interest in every person.** The more interest you show, the more wise and attractive you become to others.

- **Listen carefully** for information that can keep the conversation going.

- **Remember: People want to be with people who make them feel special,** not people who are "special." Take responsibility to help people you talk to feel as if they're the only person in the room.

- **Play the conversation game.** When someone asks, *How's business?* or *What's going on?* answer with more than *Not much.* Tell more about yourself so that others can learn more about you.

- **Be careful with business acquaintances.** You wouldn't want to open a conversation with: *How's your job at _____?* What if that person just got fired or laid off? Be careful when you're asking about an acquaintance's spouse or special friend; you could regret it.

- **Don't act like you're an FBI agent.** Questions like *What do you do?, Are you married?, Do you have children?,* and *Where are you from?* lead to dead-end conversations.

- **Be aware of body language.** Nervous or ill-at-ease people make others uncomfortable. Act confident and comfortable, even when you're not.

- **Be prepared.** Spend a few minutes before an anticipated event preparing to talk easily about three topics. They will come in handy when you find yourself in the middle of an awkward moment... or while seated at a table of eight where everyone is playing with their food.

- **Show an interest in your conversational partner's opinion, too.** You're not the only person who has opinions about funding the space program or what will happen to the stock market.

- **Stop conversation monopolists in their tracks.** If possible, wait for the person to take a breath or to pause, then break in with a comment about their topic. Immediately redirect the conversation in the direction you wish it to go.

- **Be prepared with exit lines.** You need to move around and meet others.

- **Don't melt from conversations.** Make a positive impression by shaking hands and saying goodbye as you leave.

Every encounter involves risk. As long as you keep looking for new people to meet, and you show an interest in other people, you can make friends and enjoy lively conversations.

Feel-Good Factor

P eople part with their money for two reasons: to solve a problem or to feel good about themselves. Look at it this way. It's hard to quickly evaluate the expertise of a new dentist. But you immediately know which one makes you feel more comfortable. You can take lessons from a highly qualified ski instructor. But if his silence makes you feel awkward while riding the chair lift together, you'll switch instructors. When Super K-Mart and Target carry the same items at about the same prices and they're located close together, where do you buy? You choose the store where the returns are simpler, the people are friendlier, and the appearance is cleaner — where you are made to feel more welcome.

The feel-good factor underlies every aspect of life. Even in the area of parent-teacher conferences, if your child's teacher delivers negative feedback in a way that shows empathy, not harshness, you're more likely to support the next vote to increase taxes for schools.

In a front-page story, *USA Today* reported that basketball star Kareem Abdul Jabbar hired a public-relations professional to help him get job interviews for coaching positions. Apparently, he's perceived as so aloof, he can't get high schools, colleges, or the pros to talk to him. Similarly, in the corporate world if you want a promotion but come across as aloof or reserved, you'll be overlooked in favor of someone who has warm "people skills" — skills which make others feel good about being around them.

Here's how to build rapport that leads to success in every business relationship.

- **Use small talk as a picture frame around business conversations.** Begin and end with small talk before and after making a presentation to a client, selling a widget, negotiating a contract, providing a service, or conferencing with your child's teacher. A study conducted with physicians showed those who spend a few minutes asking patients about their family, their work, or summer plans before and/or after an examination are less likely to be sued than those who don't. Let's face it. People don't sue people they care about. And we care about people who show they care about us.

- **Express empathy.** Everyone is entitled to be listened to, even when in the wrong. Consider the client who sees the stock market rise 30 percent but not his own portfolio. The stockbroker knows the client insisted on picking the stocks himself, but it would be a mistake to make the client "wrong." It's better to say, "I realize it's frustrating to experience this. What can we do from here?" That goes a long way to diffusing negative emotions and helping the client feel better about this relationship — rather than tempted to move on to another stockbroker.

- **Greet people warmly, make eye contact, and smile.** Be the first to say hello. Be careful, you might be viewed as a snob if you are not the first to say hello. People often go back to their favorite restaurants because the host greets them with a sincere smile, looks at them directly, and welcomes them with warmth. My husband and I go to our favorite restaurant — and bring our friends there, too — because the wait staff, the host/hostess, and even the owner take the time to make us feel extra special.

- **Use the person's name in conversation.** You are more likely to get special treatment by using the person's name: When you call to clarify a credit card billing, for example, say: *Joe, thanks for taking the time to help me with this question.* That makes Joe feel his role is important. If you don't know someone's name, take a moment to ask, and then repeat it. Be sure to pronounce it correctly. And never presume your conversation partner has a nickname. My name is Debra, not Debbie. I don't feel good when people call me Debbie. It's a little thing that has big importance.

- **Show an interest in others.** In response to our high-tech environment of e-mail and fax broadcasts, we need high touch more than ever. That's what you create when you show an interest in the lives of your customers/clients/patients every chance you get.

- **Dig deeper.** When you engage in a conversation, don't leave it too quickly. If your customer/client/ patient mentions her vacation, pick up on the cue and dig deeper. Ask where she went, what she did, what the highlight was, if she would go back. You'll make her feel good about her life and about taking time with you. Always follow up a question like *How's work?* with *What's been going on at work since the last time we spoke?* This way he or she knows you really want to hear about what is going on with work.

- **Be a good listener.** That means making eye contact and responding with verbal cues to show you hear what the speaker says. Verbal cues include these phrases: *Tell me more, What happened first?, What happened next?, That must have been difficult,* and so on. Using them makes people feel actively listened to.

- **Stop being an advisor.** When you mention a problem you might be having with an employee or an associate, do people offer advice without asking any questions? Have you ever put together a resume and, as soon as you sent it out, someone told you it was too long or too short or too detailed or not detailed enough? Jumping in with unsolicited advice happens annoyingly often. Instead of advice, give understanding with simple phrases like: *I know you can work out a solution* or *I hope the job hunt goes well for you.* Offer advice only when you are specifically asked for it.

An example I use in my presentations really makes my point about the feel-good factor. I wanted to find a good print shop near my home and walked into one near the busiest post office in our state. I was greeted with a sign that read: ***Lack of preparation on your part does not constitute an emergency on my part.*** I thought, how many people would zip into this shop for a few photocopies before mailing off an important package? I doubt they would feel welcome here.

I then visited a printing shop across the street. Two colorful signs posted there made my day. One featured a cactus and said, ***Stuck? We'll help you out of a prickly situation.*** The other, showing a pot of jam, read: ***In a jam? We'll help you out of a sticky situation.*** You can guess which printer made me feel better about forming a business relationship.

Whether you want to land a new job, enhance your practice, gain listings, increase your billable hours, bring new people into your business, or make sure people remember you with referrals — pay attention to the feel-good factor. And enjoy the success that follows.

Carpe Diem

As we wrap up our conversation on small talk, I am reminded of the professor in *The Wizard of Oz* after his wizardry is discovered to be hocus-pocus. The erstwhile wizard gives a provocative monologue when he tells the Lion, the Tin Man, and the Scarecrow that they already have what it is they've been seeking. All they need to do to be courageous, have a heart, or be intelligent is to claim their own skills. The Wizard merely bestows his good wishes formally.

You now have all my trade secrets right here. I have no more magic than you. You only need to continue practicing the skills, tips, and techniques demonstrated in this book. So, without further ado, I ceremoniously honor your newfound skills:

> *By the power vested in me as a former nerd who lurked in the corners when she wasn't avoiding functions altogether, who has transformed herself into a longtime successful SmallTalker, I do hereby confer upon you the title of "SmallTalker Extraordinaire."*
> *You are accorded all the rights, privileges, and responsibilities herewith. Let no party, gathering, group, or person intimidate you or squelch your conversational skills.*

You are an officially competent conversationalist. Let go of any old labels you've given yourself that stand in the way of claiming conversation as one of your strengths. The tips and tricks enumerated throughout the book are common-sense solutions to everyday small-talking dilemmas. Only one requirement is essential to achieve small talk excellence: practice. Over and over again I get confirmation about the value of small-talk skills. I hear about people whose lives have changed as dramatically as my own. A man in Florida got up the courage to ask a woman on a date, and now they're married. A woman in Ohio got promoted to head up the entire Midwest region for her company. A gentleman in his 50s in Colorado is building a new life after his wife died prematurely of cancer. She had always done all the talking for both of them.

Don't give up if you run into trouble. Calvin Coolidge once said, "Nothing in the world can take the place of persistence. Talent will not; nothing is more common than unsuccessful men of talent. Genius will not; unrewarded genius is almost a proverb. Education will not; the world is full of educated derelicts. Persistence and determination alone are omnipotent." Practice with your family and friends first and as you gain confidence, move on to business associates and other people you regularly see.

Put yourself in social situations more frequently. Accept invitations. Join a trade organization, a volunteer group, or a club. At work, volunteer for projects that will allow you to work with different people. Small-talk opportunities abound when you find yourself with strangers who share a similar passion or occupation. During the next few weeks and months, review the "Winning at Small Talk" worksheet on the following page.

I hope you're truly winning at small talk.
Fake it for a while till it becomes second nature.
If you are diligent about practicing,
you'll become an expert.

Winning at Small Talk

Please answer **Yes** or **No** to the following questions:

1. I have joined or participated in at least one club or group activity in order to develop new business friendships or meet new people.

2. I'm conscious of "taking turns" in most conversations so that I can learn more about others and help them get to know me.

3. I have used my contacts to help at least two people find new jobs, hook up with potential customers and clients, or go out on a date. I have provided information for other networking purposes.

4. I have gone to at least two functions where I can meet people in my profession/industry or who are potential decision-makers or where I can make new friends or find romance.

5. If someone is friendly toward me it is easy to be friendly back. However, I don't wait to make sure someone is friendly before I am friendly toward him or her.

6. When someone asks me, *What's new?* Instead of saying *Not much,* I often talk about something exciting in my life.

7. At meetings, parties, etc. I introduce myself to people I don't know and come away knowing the names of at least three people.